THE
DEAD
DON'T
NEED
REMINDING

The DEAD DON'T NEED REMINDING

In Search of
FUGITIVES, MISSISSIPPI,
and BLACK TV NERD SH*T

JULIAN RANDALL

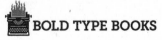

BOLD TYPE BOOKS

New York

Bold Type Books
Hachette Book Group
1290 Avenue of the Americas, New York, NY 10104
www.boldtypebooks.org
@BoldTypeBooks

Printed in the United States of America
First Edition: May 2024

Published by Bold Type Books, an imprint of Hachette Book Group, Inc. Bold Type Books is a co-publishing venture of the Type Media Center and Perseus Books.

The Hachette Speakers Bureau provides a wide range of authors for speaking events. To find out more, go to hachettespeakersbureau.com or email HachetteSpeakers@hbgusa.com.

Bold Type books may be purchased in bulk for business, educational, or promotional use. For more information, please contact your local bookseller or the Hachette Book Group Special Markets Department at special.markets@hbgusa.com.

The publisher is not responsible for websites (or their content) that are not owned by the publisher.

Editorial production by Christine Marra, *Marra*thon Production Services.
www.marrathoneditorial.org
Print book interior design by Jane Raese.
Set in 12.5-point Bodoni

Library of Congress Control Number: 2023949696

ISBNs: 9781645030263 (hardcover), 9781645030287 (ebook)

LSC-C

Printing 1, 2024

For my great grandfather,

Albert Edward Leland,

who flew.

For my father,

James Leland Randall,

who gave me my wings.

CONTENTS

The names alive are like the names in graves.

—Terrance Hayes

I know forever's a mighty long time,
so where should we begin?

—Big K.R.I.T.

THE
DEAD
DON'T
NEED
REMINDING

OXFORD

Well amen, well goddamn, Mississippi is all arrivals—
Mississippi is all beginnings.

The first time I arrive in Oxford, Mississippi, it's mid-July
and swelter jewels the kudzu with frenzied summer rains.
This is the Zero Country, I think, as the kudzu swirls over
itself like waves of water. *This is the Zero Country.* This place
that is home to some and strange to me. This is the Zero
Country, Mississippi, and I am about to take my first step
into my new life by chasing down one that ended decades
before I was born. I am looking for a particular plantation,
but, it barely registers, at the start, that Oxford is riddled
with plantation-style houses, American palaces with window
stacked upon window, every column bone-bright in the dark.

There are plantations everywhere, and they are never the
plantation I need.

It turns out, even with a northern upbringing there is no
escaping the knowledge of what a plantation house looks
like. All around, there's the dregs of one empire mimicking
another and another. Most plantation-style homes have an

almost naïve amount of windows. It's a hostile symmetry, almost violently perfect.

Hanif and I are two Black bois making our way through the dim between the streetlights pushing towards the town square, the courthouse looming up in the distance. Hanif asks me if I know how Oxford came to have so many plantation houses; they line sorority row, fraternity row, N. Lamar Street, smooth white columns everywhere gleaming. A poster celebrating Taylor Swift's new album hangs between the sorority houses. Taylor is hung up on a cross like a white feminist Jesus. I tell Hanif I don't know the answer, because I don't.

But in my heart, I feel a little nugget of shame, that I've lived three years in Oxford and I haven't spent much time thinking about where these "Greek revival" houses came from. I've been busy trying to figure out where *I* came from. I've been busy trying to figure out where I am. I'm surrounded by stories. The story of my great-grandfather whose records I came to find, the story of myself, the story of my family. And the stories that shape us. The stories we turn to out of scarcity, the cousins we make out of characters.

My story doesn't start with how Oxford got all its plantation houses, but it's as good a place as any. That story turns out to be as old as mirrors. Oxford is one empire mimicking another.

Around 1840 a young architect named William Turner strode into Oxford and began designing. He had no training. First one four-columned monstrosity, then another for the town's rich and aspiring. Every white man wanting to be exactly like the other white men, but bigger. Some things never change.

Oxford was once burned down by the Union army after the confederate soldiers, whose commemorative statue stands fourteen paces from the courthouse, refused to surrender. In the aftermath, the town square was redesigned by the architect of New Orleans, so the effect when you arrive in the town square is one of being in a miniature NOLA. Double-decker storefronts line every side of The Square, boisterous old boys cheering with full pitchers on one balcony, blond-bright girls in shimmering ball gowns on the way to a sorority formal passing below.

I'm staring at the cadre of white boys making their way up the street when Hanif lets me know he's probably headed off to his hotel for the night. I nod and we're making our way under the unblinking eyes of the confederate soldier at the top of his stone column when a small flash of green catches my eye. I nudge my head to the side and Hanif follows me to the monument so I can show him one of the strangest things about living in Oxford. Every Sunday, rain or shine, I find a mint-green copy of the complete speeches of Martin Luther King Jr. at the foot of the statue. Sometimes it is in a Ziploc bag, sometimes it's the only color in the stone. Sometimes me and the picture of Dr. King, who looks equally unamused on the cover of his collected speeches, are the only Black on The Square. I find the speeches because I make a weekly trip to The Square to shop for books and spit on that same statue as hard as I can. I suppose we all have our subversions, none of mine have brought the statue down.

I do and don't know what I am trying to prove.

I am in Oxford for an MFA. My mother told me not to die here. I'm only here because of a story, but my mother knows stories can be lethal.

My family left Mississippi during the Great Migration. Some days, the hope of finding my relatives' graves, the records of their flights and escapes is all that keeps me on this earth. I am looking for their plantations, their gravestones, their memory. All I find is confederate soldiers instead.

I rarely see myself anywhere. Hanif leaves and it is only me and the faded memory of Martin Luther King Jr. on the town square.

This is a book that contains two stories I can't stop telling. One is about my great-grandfather. The other is about who I became in pursuit of the fugitive who once cradled my grandmother as a baby, stories about invisibility, about Black TV nerd shit and the cousins we make from scarcity. I'll tell you one by telling you the other, but I think the moral of both is that there's nothing Blacker than uncertainty.

Mississippi is all arrivals. Mississippi is all beginnings.

But Mississippi is also something we return to, again and again, to find where we started in hopes of catching a glimpse of how we might end.

❧

THE BOOK OF Martin Luther King Jr. speeches is the only color in the stone on a night where I'm dancing as if nothing has ever touched me or will again. Within Proud Larry's, a low-slung multi-room bar of dark wood and yawning floorboards off S. Lamar Street, there's a party that only happens once or twice a semester that has pulled me out of the crib. A Code Pink party, a queer space that only blooms at night, and tonight I'm a *Gardenia augusta* in a forest of boys I may never see again; in the right moonlight I blossom into a field of surrenders.

The last time I promised my mother I wouldn't die here, it was the first time as well. I promised I wouldn't draw attention to myself and my understanding of my sexuality, I promised in essence not to be touched and so I wasn't. Whatever dancing I do, it is almost always with myself. Even when I am killing it, and in Oxford I am considered a much better dancer than I am literally anywhere else, I am often courting the intimacy of audience, not friends. I want the space between us jeweled with pulsing lights, but don't get it twisted—I want that space between us.

And so I am once again garden unto myself, little Eden, ruined once and holy for never having been touched again. But then, I am touched. And it is the arms of a boy dark as me, the blue light thrumming between us & we could pass for *Moonlight*, or we could pass for moonlight, but the space between us electric with the need that crests in every high note. I am against his chest, hips churning, and still word for word with the SZA track my DJ homie put in queue because she knows if you play "The Weekend" by SZA I dance like I still have two good knees and we are all due a vacation from our pains and our promises.

But just like that, the boy is gone. And I'm not heart-broken, just myself. I'm dancing among my homies from the English and Southern Studies department. Eventually I get tired, I'm ready to go home but I walked the mile and a half here thinking I'd hold the wall until my homegirl's set was up and bounce. But I've danced too hard, been too free and as usual the price is paid in my tendons, a pound of flesh pulled too thin until the pain is almost a music of its own. But my homegirl whose DJing is a little tipsy is not ready to leave. Luckily, unluckily, a boy I know from school offers me a ride. I feel grateful I don't have to walk all the way back down Jackson ave. The bass swallows some of our words, I don't realize that he never offered to take me home.

We are halfway up Jackson ave when my ears adjust back from the bass, just in time for a sped-up sample of "Party in the U.S.A." to hit me full in the face outside a bar called Funky's, where teens go to drink with their recently non-teen homies. The boy who offered me a ride but not to take me home is pointing to one of his students, bent over with a not small amount of vomit on a pair of sneakers I'm sure cost half my rent. I ask how far to the car and the boy stops still for the first time. The smell of police horses wafts in the May wind, the condensation of the morning settling along my forearms. These are the things I remember later when I realize that the boy was making a move all along. He asks what I thought this was and I open my mouth, but there is nothing to say besides that I don't see him that way. Asking if he would still be down to give me a ride home goes . . . about as well as you'd expect. I can already feel the ache that'll settle

into the torn spot in my groin, sharp with protest, gearing up
for a long walk, unironically uphill both ways.

Or, it would have been. But I saw a group of six Black
boys in what was, unmistakably, about to be a fight with three
profoundly drunk white boys and two very drunk white girls.
And I know, the walk ahead of me down Jackson ave is long
and growing longer with every minute that I am feeling my
knees swell—but something like love makes me cross the
street to try and pull them away before shit gets out of hand.
Something like memory makes me eye the police horses, advancing up the block slowly, the grim hands of their riders
bone-bright as the knuckles of a plantation house and this
too, a memory.

Here's what I know about what started the fight that night:

1. The Black boys saw out of the corner of their eye that
   one drunken white boy out of the cadre was yanking
   his girlfriend around harshly. They asked if she was
   OK, she said yes. He pushed her again, hard, seconds
   later, so they ask the bleach-blond white girl again if
   she is OK, since he was squeezing the blood from her
   wrist.

2. Annoyed, the white girl said, "Nigger, I've got this."

3. All hell broke loose.

4. I arrived as White Boy #1 was shoving against the
   other two white boys, trying to leap into the arms

of the six Black boys, all of whom are holding the other back from throwing the first punch at a white boy who looks like he comes from a long line of first punches.

5. The second white girl, sorority shirt billowing white as a Rain Lily, in an attempt to defuse the situation that her abused homegirl had just escalated, began rapidly introducing herself to everyone in the circle, her hand wilting in the space between when no one reached back out.

The Black boys are telling me all of this when one of us towards the back cries out that it's happening again behind us. And we are turning as one to see White Boy #1, who has just finished bodily hurling his girl into the grassy hillside of the courthouse, her face landing inches from a set of harsh concrete steps. I don't remember deciding to go back, I remember seeing the police horses, slowed by a small tide of undergrads reaching out to pet them. I remember hollerin, "Motherfucker, don't you fuckin touch her. We don't do that shit here." All of this has passed in a second, and then another, when I pull my eye from the slowly advancing police horses to see that the white girl has groggily climbed the steps behind her abuser. Almost in slow motion, I watch her launch from atop the steps, fist cocked back and screaming, "Motherfucker" in a way that's maybe a word but undeniably a howl.

I don't want metaphor for this. I don't want music for this. I do not want to use language to turn the white girl into anything but what she was, a girl in the air and then a girl with a fist exploding up through her chin. I have still never seen anyone get hit that hard in my entire life. I watched all the momentum leave her body, then watched in horror as she arched backwards, head pointed towards the concrete steps. And there was no line between silence and noise, I do not know if I said, "Dear god, I think he just killed her" or if it was merely the loudest and only thought in my head as she rag-dolled into the grassy hill, the concrete inches from her face.

The last time I saw that man he was in handcuffs, not for that hit, but the one that came after. When the girl struggled once again to her feet and the officers finally saw her from atop their horses, when they cuffed the man and he said not "sorry," or "I didn't mean to," and not even choosing to say nothing. He simply rose from the pavement, still handcuffed, and began walking down the street before telling the officer that he was "bored." The last time I saw that man, we were all of us Black bois riding back down Jackson ave past the sign that marks Freedmen's Town, evergreen as a southern oak. Dogwoods yawned against each other, mosquitoes feasted, Code Pink came to a close with a host of boys gladly in the arms of another.

Mississippi stayed Mississippi; everything and nothing had changed.

EVERYTHING AND NOTHING had changed the day my literary agent called to tell me this book wasn't happening. Or, rather, that our last best hope had collapsed. It is June, and I am tired of too many things to count. It had been nearly a year of trying to sell this collection, and the last editor, whose most memorable feedback was *"That train you wanted to jump in front of might not've killed you, it might've just made you wish you were dead"* is now insisting on turning this book into a memoir about a life I almost gave up. So there I sit in the shadow of Oxford city hall, holding the phone and wondering if it's worth bothering the expert I came here to interview, now that even a bad door won't open.

Rhondalyn K. Peairs and I meet anyway on the balcony of Square Books, where she's been waiting for me. Rhondalyn's voice is a warm stretch, every other syllable sprawling into a deeply southern music; she seems at ease in the Mississippi summer, which makes perfect sense given that she's in her hometown.

Back since 2008, Rhondalyn has been one of Oxford's most prominent historians and the founder of HISTORICH, a tour service that specifically highlights the history, works, and spaces of Black folks in Oxford and Lafayette County at large. We sit a spell and talk on how often the histories of Black folks in the county are hidden in plain sight.

So much so that I learned early in the conversation that even after three and a half years, I hadn't known Molly Barr Road was named after a Black woman. Not only that, but that Molly Barr was a contemporary superhero who bought up long tracts of land in developing Oxford before the town was really the town. Long tracts of land that she then cleanly divided into homesteads of Black families looking to make cul-de-sacs and hamlets of free Black people, built around schools and churches.

Coming up in Chicago, I was used to the story of how Black people came to congregate in a place to be as much a matter of public policy as it was a matter of joy. I spent as much of my time wondering where Black people "were" as being around Black people. I wondered if I had failed for having only really found a home in Goolsby's barbershop, but Rhondalyn lets out a small laugh, cool as July rain.

"Nah, it's pretty endemic, the city doesn't do a good job at all connecting the histories or telling the stories they can." She shrugs.

And it's true, I went all this time not knowing the churches and only seeing the pockets from beyond the window of a Blue Line bus I'd been riding three stops too long past where I was aiming. As people walk up and around The Square and from the corner of my eye, I can see the book of King's speeches, a dry mint-green seed at the base of the confederate statue. We sit a spell longer and Rhondalyn asks me a question I get a lot: "What are you doing in Mississippi?" I tell her I came looking for the truest story I know about a man threatened with wings. I know this is not *my* home, but it is sometimes *a* home to me. It's become a place I know in my bones, in a way I will always belong best to this light, this Mississippi light that clings just so to the dogwoods and pine. We laugh and trade stories until I almost forget that the book I'm interviewing her for may never exist. I'm just glad to learn something about Oxford, this town where I taught myself to live again.

WELL AMEN, WELL goddamn, another beginning.

#JULIAN4SPIDERMAN

OK, people, let's do this one last time.

Spider-Man has always been Black.

In this universe he's me. I am six years old and posted up in front of the TV before my first Halloween party. The costume is perfect except for the mask; it's made for everyone but also it isn't. Beneath the mask my head looks off-kilter, asymmetrical, as if drawn by someone only half interested. My hair, like my mother's hair and her mother's before her, swells in pitch-black waves like I am told the ocean looks some nights in DR. I slick my small hands along the top of the mask, feel the pinpoints of hair poking through. For the first time I feel powerful and unmanageable at once. I am stubble insisting through the polyester—new grass in a country of no rain.

The truth is I can't see shit out of the mask.

There are eyeholes, but they're narrow. I keep tugging until finally they open, and the mask weeps. You can see my eyes, and the deep brown skin that rings them. This becomes typical; the consequence of being seen is that you're seen. My parents, afraid to look like they bought me a crappy costume in front of the other parents, decide to scrap the mask altogether.

I sit war-paint still in the bathroom as my mother details in the web lines along my face, fills the red to blush between, drapes my eyelids with enough white. It's some of her finest work. It's my favorite thing and the only thing I have ever seen her paint. I look in the mirror. I want you to feel what I did as I touched the long web over my mouth, my cheeks, stopping at my hairline. I felt like a map to a city I'd never seen but always lived in. I stood between my parents in the mirror and I smiled until the paint nearly cracked. I'm their son, I'm Spider-Man, I'm me. This is my universe. Everyone knows what I am. The mask is perfect because I am no longer underneath it.

❦

OK, people, let's do this one more time.

Spider-Man has always been Black—but he hasn't always been Spider-Man.

In this universe Spider-Man's name is Miles Morales and I don't remember how old I was the first time I was asked, "What are you?"

In this universe Miles and I are both Black and Latinx, Peter Parker is dead and Miles has gathered for the funeral with the rest of New York. This is our universe where my parents must have been in love once. In this universe Miles has been bitten, Miles has powers, Miles is Spider-Man, but not quite yet. The mask sags at his eyes, his brown skin is two perfect rings; he can see, but doesn't know where to go. The costume doesn't fit in the way most things don't fit in middle school, though we are told that it always fits eventually. Everyone is counting on Miles but only he knows it. In this way we are the same boy.

I don't remember how old I was the first time I was asked, "What are you?" I know that Miles, like any of the other boys like us, must wish, truly, that he was explaining who he was and what was going on one last time and could mean it. Origin stories are frustrating in this way, a gravity we are pulled and pulled to—many Spider-Verses, but always the same violences.

So here is mine. My father is Black and from St. Louis, though around strangers he will say he is from Manhattan because sometimes we are from where we were least dead and not where we were born. My mother is Dominican and from Washington Heights, born and raised by parents who escaped the Trujillato. My parents have been alive together since the eighties, they've been alive together all my life. This is my origin as far as I can follow it: they met in New York and loved each other, and when I was born they loved each other anywhere else but especially in Chicago. This is where I best like to remember them: as young and lucky as they will ever be in my memory, grief less legible on all our faces than it is now.

Miles, like me, is made of questions, maybe most of all about his name. There are a number of theories around the origin of Miles's name. They range from "affirmative action" to "progress narrative."

In *Into the Spider-Verse*, Miles's father is a Black man named Jefferson Davis, and in our universe he is voiced by Brian Tyree Henry. Miles's mother is a Puerto Rican woman named Rio Morales, voiced by Lauren Vélez, another language whispering beneath her few lines, a dance only shadows are fluent in. Like my mother she is quiet. My mother, who acts as my father's translator even when everyone is speaking English.

I have become accustomed to correcting my name in other people's mouths because this is a blunt-tongued country. It's a reflex. Asking strangers to smooth the *J* to an *H*. But it's not a hard name, I promise. My father wanted another *J*, my mother wanted something Spanish. They were looking for a name that white people couldn't mistake for their own son. Obscurity is both an inheritance and a superpower, it turns out.

OK, people, let's do this one more time.

Spider-Man has always been Black.

Before there was Miles Morales there was Peter Parker, and before there was Peter Parker there was Anansi, the Spider Man.

The first Spider Man was a storyteller. The first storyteller.

I learned this from my father, who read Anansi's origin to me every night. Anansi's origin is called simply *A Story, a Story*. It's a children's book about how Anansi, small and clever, outwitted the most dangerous creatures in the world so he could buy the stories of the world from the sky-god Nyame. I didn't know then that this story, this power, was how my father had managed to survive long enough to make me. My massive deep-voiced protector, spinning a tale he had probably been nursing all day in the back of his mind as he went through the motions of his corporate job.

At the mostly white school he sends me to, I do what children do: I mimic. I tell the story of the first Spider Man and folks were mostly confused. Spider-Man is white, everybody knows that. I grow quieter the older my small body becomes. I am invisible in stretches I can never predict. I negotiate and I trick and I pretend like my father, like Anansi. I learn to code-switch, some strange compromise between fight and flight. This camouflage becomes my voice, this mask becomes my face. I go to school in Chicago and Omaha and Philly and Minneapolis and always somewhere I don't belong, somewhere where it is safer to be no one.

My parents are counting on me, like Miles's parents are counting on him. They believe that I am the best of them. Like Miles, all I want to do is escape back to what I know. I try, many times, to scale the fence at recess so I can sneak away, go home, to where I am seen, loved. I fall each time because I don't have the strength to leave silence. I am a dark outline, a skyline of expectations happening to either side of my brief body. I am Spider-Man, but I'm not yet. I am me, but not quite. The other kids' parents ask, "What are you?" I find ways to tell the story until I don't even notice how often in a day I use the word "half." I don't notice how much I believe it. I don't know the price of power, but I know that I want whatever can allow me to be away; whatever story is the price for that I chameleon into.

Clever Boy.

Clever Spider using his mouth to throw punches at the sky.

ℜ

OK, people, let's do this one more time.

Before Spider-Man was Spider-Man he was a scholarship student. This is the story of two Spider-Men in 2018 and 2006, respectively.

In 2018 Miles Morales is on-screen and staring down the barrel of a zero out of one hundred on a test. I know exactly what this is. Miles's teacher thinks she does too. She says, "You're trying to quit and I'm not going to let you." All the hairs on the back of my neck stand up, my sixth sense on red alert. Call it déjà vu, or Spidey Sense, call it memory or trigger, the end result is that I remember. Without my noticing, my knuckles congeal to fists, my mouth goes dry because I have been here before. An origin story is another way of saying "beginning," when and where we begin to learn. Lesson 1: Don't watch the mouth, watch the hands.

I've never read *Great Expectations*, but I *have* been assigned essays to make sure I was as smart as advertised.

In the winter of 2006, in Chicago, my history teacher tasks me with arguing in favor of slavery. He doesn't call it that, at first, but I know power when I see it. We are in one of my favorite rooms in the school. Mr. Stone was a short white boy from Boston who kept a recreation of the Last Supper in which all of the disciples and Jesus himself are Black. I stared at Black Jesus when I couldn't look into Mr. Stone's eyes as he hurt me. Months later Stone will tell my father that he thinks I'm trying to quit, and that he's not going to let me.

We are in the room because I'm asking to be switched off the states' rights side of a Civil War debate. My memory sputters when I try to recall whether there was another Black kid in the class; what I remember is that I was the only one who was asked. Ordinarily in class I am quiet, but I beg him not to make me do this. I am not tall and never will be. Beyond the window in this universe it is maybe snowing and maybe not. My body is swimming in a graffitied Ecko Unltd. hoodie and my chest is draped with a tiny Phat Farm chain that looks like it came out of an egg machine, even though I spent all the money I had just to hold its shine. I flit in and out of visibility, my hair muzzled by a camouflage Chicago Bears hat I have been wearing every day since I started living only with my father. I have gotten good at pretending, I know to stare at someone's hair so it can be mistaken for eye contact. I notice that Mr. Stone has my mother's hair as he tells me that arguing against slavery "wouldn't be enough of a challenge" for a student "like you."

Miles's teacher says that the only way for a person to get everything wrong is to know how to get everything right. I don't know if this is true. What I do know is that a week later I am in class sitting behind a sign that says "States' Rights," dodging sneak attack after sneak attack as the pro-abolition group comes after me and not the other two kids on my panel. I grow quieter because I am trying to argue against myself. I flit in and out of visibility until Mr. Stone stops the debate and admonishes the class. "Julian is up here arguing for slavery," he says. "What's your excuse?" Invisibility can be suffocating. Invisibility can be your only refuge. Like every refuge, invisibility can be taken away. The consequence of being seen is that you're seen.

The only way for a person to get everything wrong is to know how to get everything right. I don't know if this is true. But I know that as Chicago's wind ballooned my Ecko jacket behind me and suspicious eyes trailed me through Lincoln Park as I walked home, I was dressed like one expectation. The outfit of a larger person I would never become rippled in the wind. I was not large enough for any of the expectations of my body and was somehow dying of all of them at once. I decide to start getting it wrong, to stop trying. "Trying" landed me arguing for my own destruction. I watch my grades slip on purpose until even I believe it is because I am not equal to the work. My classmates call me a half-breed and I don't know how to correct them because I have learned that Half is my name.

I never tell Mr. Stone that this is when I stopped trusting him. I smile and pretend I just don't understand. I never tell him that sometimes I wonder what the difference is between wanting to quit and wanting to go home. This is my universe and nobody knows what I am until it is time to punish me. All my teachers know something is wrong, they just don't know that they are what's wrong. The rest of the school year my fists are knotted in my pockets until they cramp. Don't watch the mouth, watch the hands.

᪣

OK, people, let's do this one more time.

Spider-Man has always been Black, but nobody knows who he is.

I didn't hear the word "Afro-Latino" until I was already in college. By this time I am nineteen and ragged, glitching in a universe that is not my own. It's hard to make friendships in the Latinx students' group; there are one or two ways to be "Latinx enough" and a multiverse of ways to be an exile. Despite the best efforts of an Afro-Latinx president, other students speak Spanish about me, in front of me, as if I can't hear them. Because I admit I am not fluent, because I tell them I am not from either of the coasts but from Chicago, because my performance of Latinidad is inherently Black, because one of the senior Latinx students who is a role model of mine starts calling me "Blackface," maybe for all of these reasons or none of them, I'm invisible again. This never changes, nobody ever apologizes.

We never see Miles have a crisis on-screen about being Black and Latinx. Never see him grinding his teeth at another "What are you?" Miles is always resolutely aware that he doesn't have to prove his Latinidad to anyone, and this is one of my favorite parts. Sometimes I wonder if this is his least believable power.

In the few meetings I drag myself to, words like "we" and "us" are thrown around, and I'd be lying if I said it wasn't seductive, isn't still seductive, this notion of a "we." Wouldn't it be nice to be part of such a web, a single story. Nobody says "anti-Blackness," they say racism as if it is not theirs too.

It is understood for years in Latinx spaces that I am "so-and-so's Black friend." This is true at every tour stop with my best friend where the Latinx professors generally engage with him alone. It's true in every Latinx Studies course I will take for the entirety of my undergraduate career. It is what folks hold true in the campus spaces where Latinx narratives are dangerously flattened and Blackness is treated as a disqualifier for Latinidad.

It's not true. But you could have fooled me.

The night someone asks me if I am Afro-Latinx for the first time I don't feel like a "half." Until then it had seemed as if there were some crucial parts of being Latinx that I had gotten wrong, always slow on the draw to my own identity.

Miles Morales has existed in my universe for a little over a year by this point, and because I want to hold on to this feeling I tweet out "#Julian4Spiderman."

OK, people, let's do this one more time.

Spider-Man has always been Black and part of being Spider-Man is that there are long silences between you and who you love.

I'm depressed in my dorm room, ignoring a call from my dad, and it goes to voicemail. Every bed I'm in feels as though I have been tied to it. No matter how I enter a room, it feels as though I have been left behind in it. I would say it's an ungodly hour but anyone who's been depressed knows that, in the midst of an episode, they are all ungodly hours.

I don't have the strength to leave silence, silence has no interest in leaving me. How do you explain to someone you love how often your greatest nemesis lives in your head? That sometimes it feels as though you are the mask? That it has been such a long time since you heard yourself speak that you're not sure what your voice sounds like anymore, that past a certain point even sounds become invisible? That it can be like this for weeks, that a month all but disappears and you don't know how?

For most of *Spider-Verse*, Miles's parents have no idea where he is.

He is the son believing that whatever is changing in him is too much danger for his family to bear, and they are the parents believing the most dangerous change is how easily their boy now inflicts his invisibility on them. Miles's father leaves message after message, they stack and blink in Miles's phone just like mine.

An interesting thing about *Spider-Verse* is that Miles Morales is slow by design. Miles is initially animated at twelve frames per second, unlike nearly everything else in his world, which moves at a standard twenty-four frames per second. Depression feels like this to me, the world happening faster than I can conceive of moving to catch up to it. How much whirred past me while I listened to the phone buzz as if it were on the other side of the door? While I heard the invariable pattern of my father finding new ways to say "I'm worried"?

The shape of my father's voicemails never changes; it's one of innumerable things I love about him. He always starts, "Hey, Julian, it's your dad." As if he is not the only person who still leaves me voicemails. He tells me, even when I have disappeared for days, weeks, that he is proud of me, that I am his son. I try not to forget to be grateful for these messages when the world is moving faster and I don't have the strength to keep up. I forget anyway. This is why, when Miles's father says, "I see this spark in you, it's amazing, it's why I push you, but it's yours, whatever you choose to do with it you'll be great," I am back in 2015 and I am standing on a street corner in Philly, as my father tells me:

"I am sorry if I have failed you. No matter who you want to be, I know you'll be the best at it. I love you, nothing will ever stop that, do you believe me?"

How long had the danger been building in me that I'd let him think I could ever forget that?

ॐ

OK. People, let's do this for the last time.

Sometimes the only cure for danger is to become more dangerous.

Miles, in his universe, is suspended between skyline and ground, pulling the window behind him, each shard making a sky full of daggers. I always close my eyes in the moment when Miles hurtles, eyes narrowing, towards the ground; it is the moment where the boy we are becomes something constant across all universes.

I, too, in my saddest hours, have looked out the window and told myself a hundred stories about falling.

Afro-Latinx life is this in so many ways: to be taught that you are dangerous, and shameful and difficult to imagine.

"Faith" is a slippery word. But there's a moment at exactly 1:24:06 when Miles's web connects to the building he leapt from and the body jerks into another kind of flight. The instant right after this one is when I close my eyes. Each time I call out alongside Blackway: "CAN'T STOP ME NOW!"

I don't know much about faith, but I know it feels like that—being Afro-Latinx feels like this. And maybe it is the irony that I love best, that I see myself best sometimes with my eyes closed and a song beckoning danger, how I know the drums in my blood and know the boy who bargained with the sky-gods to own *A Story* will rise each time.

The moment Miles Morales becomes Spider-Man is more than the end to a hero's journey: every time I watch it I am gifted back to myself.

Spider-Man in a hoodie and Jordans. Spider-Man in the city where my parents fell in love. Spider-Man in the place where none of us died. The voices that follow Miles as he swings into his new life, into full command of his powers, are the voices of my family. Representation matters, but this is more than that, too. It is one thing to have spent too much of a life begging to be seen, describing myself as "half." It is another thing entirely to imagine myself, mid-leap, all the noise of a city below me and expect, finally, to live.

Miles pulls the mask away to reveal his face and I am six again, Spider-Man's face is my face, and I remember that it has always been this way. On opposite sides of the screen we are both wearing the half-grins of someone who could have died but didn't. We exist, and there is no need to explain. Spider-Man has always been Black, and we're not half of anything.

WATER VALLEY

By dark, the letters in the hill are the only light for what feels like miles. Were it not for the lights planted in front of them, you could mistake the letters for an abundance of flowers, petals uniformly the color of surrender. They sit, cotton-white in a dark green hill, announcing the border into the town where my family was once likely enslaved. This is Water Valley, Mississippi; this is the Zero Country, the beginning of the story or at least as far back as I could trace it.

It is 2017: me and my roommate Joshua have piled into the car, since we have both been summoned to be readers at the opening of Mississippi's only queer feminist bookstore. I'm peering out the window rotating the word "escape" in my mind. The sun pulls low, floods the fields I imagine our hands tended once. Ya boi sees it as clear as any time in my life that there can never be enough miles between you and the memory of bondage but here I am, watching the miles wilt between me and where, allegedly, Albert Leland was once a child who grew into a single pair of pearl-white wings.

Reports diverge on where my great-grandfather was born and they diverge because his birthday was mostly guess-work. If there was a record in the town of Water Valley on how long Albert Leland was ever a child, I have not found it. But in 2017 I intend to finally lay eyes on the town that pops up on my dad's ancestry.com when we ask where Albert Leland definitely met Jeanette Wheelis, my great-grand-mother. This was our south, our Zero Country—we weren't from a place, we were from an event and we'd been running ever since.

It's hard not to be seduced by the irony of the situation. That the first time I'm arriving somewhere that it was once openly illegal for Black people, including my own family, to be literate is to read poems at the opening of a bookstore that many folks in the town wish had never existed. That night, a man will experience a small heatstroke in the back of the audience and the event will end with me and Joshua piling back into his car, the dark already knit over the re-maining architecture of Main Street. I watch the legend fade until only the moon remains in pursuit. I'd thought there'd be more daylight; like always, I thought I had more time. For my next planned visit, I know I'll have to rent a Zipcar—with money that I don't really have to go to a town that does not want me there. I will think about inheritance and what I want to learn. When I return a little over a month later, I will learn almost nothing, because ash has no memory; because heat holds no allegiance.

The morning I arrive in Water Valley for the second time, I cleared the day to go and have a conversation with

the archivist at city hall. The honeyed light of midday floods
the main street of the town and I notice all over again how
Mississippi shares its flat nature with Chicago—how you can
look casually and see for something like forever.

I call city hall and get a message that they're out for
lunch, so I make my way into a bar a little way down from
the railroad museum and see a flag that I would've thought
was for Texas, if not for the magnolia tree flaring out against
a stark white background. And look, I'm not one to weep for
flags; I'm still not. But I've wept over a life denied before, and
whenever I have imagined my grandmother's first steps in
Greenville, some of her last ever in Mississippi, it is always
beneath a mythically large magnolia tree and every heady
blossom blooms from grenade to bell to bride; and it is the
second slowest surrender in all of Mississippi. And the only
Mississippi flag I'd ever known had a confederate flag tucked
in the eye of it and it had flown since 1894 to stop some
confederate veterans from doing what confederate soldiers
are for. Flown since the first time my grandmother would
have been able to point a child's finger to all thirteen stars
and learn that they all hated her equally. I wanted a life for
her beneath that magnolia tree, I wanted every generous star
within reach.

The man seated beneath the flag knows I'm not from
around here. He asks what I'm doing in Mississippi and I
tell him I came looking for a man swallowed in the drawl of
June. When I asked the man next to me what the flag was
of, he blinked and said, "Mississippi" and didn't elaborate.
And maybe that's because the flag was . . . something of a

"limited edition." According to Mississippi governor John
M. Stone in 1894, the magnolia flag only ran from 1861 to
1865, a period in which famously nothing of any import at
all happened in the state of Mississippi, of course. Stone
hilariously only mentions the flag was commissioned at a
"State Convention" in 1861 (Secession a.k.a. Grand Opening) and then decommissioned at a separate "State Convention" in 1865 (Surrender to the Union Army a.k.a. Grand
Closing).

But it is years before I learn this, years before the final
state flag to hold the confederate battle symbol comes down
for the last time because George Floyd was murdered and we
trade Black death for symbols all the time in America. The
magnolia blooms still on flags across the state; some with
trees, some without.

And still, when I imagine my grandmother fleeing the
only home she'd ever known, just for a moment all the magnolia petals perfume the wind-churn until, like her father,
they are almost-feathers, almost-birds.

I can't know if there was ever a tree, only that grief makes
me wonder a number of things I can now never ask. Among
them, if me and my grandmother shared a favorite flower,
their petals' aroma thickening the late Mississippi sky until
you can barely smell the ash.

The daylight sags into violet by the time I step out of the
bar. I figure that enough time has passed, so I put my headphones back on and walk the streets towards a city hall that
is at once a clerk's office, city hall and a fire station—all
piled into one ruddy brick building, barely taller than me.

And I know there must be a story there, and I know in a deeper place in my marrow that I'm on the wrong side of it.

I was right.

Within a year of my great-grandfather taking Jeanette Wheelis's hand, the two had already begun to plot their way towards a town to the south called Greenville. I can't know what was said, but where I don't know I like to imagine. What I imagine is that Albert Leland clasped the hand of his wife and told her his plan to run his hustle for as long as the hustle was feeling generous with him. Magnolias swayed everywhere, the whole state dressed for a wedding or a surrender.

And so it was that my grandmother years later would be born in the blade of the Cleaver state, with a blues already coiling over her head. Within a year of my great-grandfather leaving Water Valley, the city hall of Water Valley burned down to the ground. One month later, the city clerk's office went the same way.

The city clerk says this to me gently in 2017, as if she is telling me someone has died. Even though, in a way, that is what I came to tell her.

The way back home to Oxford is wreathed with flames, an amnesia in the midst of swelter. I'm almost mad I didn't see it coming, furious to find that the way back may simply not exist. I take one last look over my shoulder before I climb back in the Zipcar that's due in an hour. I imagine a bouquet of flame swallowing the building, and I drive back towards the town I call my home even though it is lousy with plantations.

All the architecture agrees, a bad thing happened here. I don't agree about what the bad thing was.

The
BOJACK HORSEMAN
STORY

EXT. Therapist's Office

The year *BoJack Horseman* premiered, I sprinted out of a therapist's office; my world had begun to disintegrate into a series of jump cuts. I called them "jump cuts" because, at least in my head, it sounded less alarming than someone with a near-perfect memory finding themselves in rooms they didn't remember walking into. It had begun junior year, maybe even in the fever that was my sophomore year, but nobody was keeping count, least of all me.

All I knew for sure was that I was definitely verging into something more than the "normal sad" I'd come to rely on. Me and my brain had an uneasy peace going, or I at least thought we did. But these prolonged dissociations, the film bubbling at the edges of my memory, were a clear breach of the fucking roommate guidelines.

I didn't know how to call what was happening "dissociation" because vocabulary is a privilege. When a friend suggested I visit counseling services on Swarthmore's campus, my mind drifted briefly to the only person I'd ever seen in therapy, Tony Soprano. Then to a couple of folks I'd hung with freshman year, then a girl I met at Bryn Mawr during one of the two classes I was taking off campus that semester. White, all white. And white in a way that, even in my lil private-school-privilege adjacency, I couldn't make heads or tails of. But still I went, because I was terrified that something was really wrong with me. And I sprinted out for the same reason.

Mental health is a journey. I began mine by staring down a faux-wood hallway, row upon row of olive-green doors stretched surreally before me. And at the end of that hallway? I'm not sure. There's another jump cut and I am watching myself whirl on my heels and slam through double doors into the air. I'm twenty, and maybe if I'm lucky I will pass from this world before someone with a degree can tell me that this feverish sadness isn't a season, it's me. It was always me.

INT. The Old Sugarman Place

On the way to my grandmother's funeral, me and my father drive through a place that should've been his. It is 2020 and the sun is yawning over us on our way down. We are going to Calvary Cemetery in St. Louis, where Dorothy Mae Leland Randall is scheduled to be buried. I hadn't known that my grandmother could die. After my grandfather passed, while my dad was a junior in college, she'd been the only parent he had left and she'd never made it much of a secret that she didn't want him.

For much of my life, it was as simple as that. Simple as watching her dazed and vicious berating of my father for hours over the phone about money she could have sworn he'd stolen, money that was sometimes still in her hand. I knew from the time I was young that when she called, things got worse. I loved her, but at times that love was more an obligation, more a by-product of feeling I didn't have the right to hate a woman who couldn't remember to be unkind to me, only him.

In the fourth season of *BoJack Horseman*, the incredibly depressed main character, BoJack, watches a group of fellow horses running shirtless beneath a relentless sun. He is fresh off a bender that ended in the overdose death of the girl who played his adoptive TV daughter on *Horsin' Around*, Sarah Lynn. He has hit one of many rock bottoms he'll face over the course of the show. So, he does what depressed people do. He ignores his friends' calls, he disappears even to himself, he runs without a destination. Finally inspired by a childhood image of his mother, Beatrice Horseman, BoJack hightails it to Michigan as depressed niggas are wont to do in times of crisis.

I've only ever seen one photo of my grandma as a baby, and even now it sometimes feels surreal to consider that she was once a child. In the picture her face is full of a joy that I want to say I only saw a few times in the twenty-six years we were both alive, but truthfully I don't know that I ever did. Like BoJack, I followed a long trail to try and find proof that my grandmother was, somewhere in Mississippi, a child like any other child.

In "The Old Sugarman Place," BoJack struggles to try and fix up his family's old vacation home. BoJack is huddled under a blanket watching TV on his phone because he can't figure out how to make his own house into somewhere he won't freeze to death. Once again I'm relating to some shit I shouldn't be able to relate to.

But I relate anyway. The house remembers a child Beatrice whose mother went sick with grief after her All-American older brother, Crackerjack, was killed by Nazis in World War II. I think of my grandmother. I realize there might have been days, years, during which that baby, born at the beginning of an endless Mississippi summer, lived happily. That she must have taken her first steps unconcerned with whether or not she was a white man's daughter. That baby, my grandmother, formed her first memories somewhere. She formed her next memories in a place to which she was told she could never return. A place two hours by car from where I sat watching "The Old Sugarman Place" the day it premiered.

In watching that episode I am watching something like her memories, though they were scattered long before I knew to ask about this story. I'm ashamed, at some level, it took this long to consider that my great-grandfather's flight from Greenville was to have every childhood comfort ripped away from her in the way Beatrice Horseman watched everything she treasured about her girlhood crumble behind her. I never thought to ask as a child what happened to her between the baby picture and a soft-lit photo of her draped in red at twenty years old, the prettiest girl in all East St. Louis. What had those years done to the daughter she was, the daughter I never grew to be.

On the way to her funeral, I am listening to my father, who is pointing to a couple of storefronts on the side of the road. He is telling me that, before he died, my grandfather had purchased that stretch of road. He'd named it Skipper-ville, after my dad's childhood church nickname. My father is pointing and I'm rewinding the clock in my head, prying the stores apart board by board until there is nothing but pavement. I'm doing this as my father tells me that it took months for him to learn that his mother, my grandmother, had sold it out from under him, shortly after his dad died. And just like that, it's the present again. My grandmother is dead, and everything is different now. Every story about grief is also a story about time.

INT. Therapist's Office

I let it slip to my first therapist that I see myself as having been born broken. But ya boi has been broken on more than one occasion, and I wonder how many times you can break a broken thing until there isn't much point to calling that shit by its name.

In the moment I was just trying to fall out of love with the idea that I'd ever been "normal," that "normal" was a place, like Mississippi, that could be returned to. That's all I'd really wanted, to feel that the words I'd started using for myself, like "depression," "anxiety," "panic attacks," were just therapy-speak. And that, like terms I'd learned in college—"p-value," "Natty Lite," "meal plus points"—there would come a point where I just wouldn't need them anymore. I wanted Keisha the therapist to tell me that, and if she couldn't tell me that, I wanted her to be impressed by the idea of all the shit I could do if there weren't days and weeks when I could barely summon the desire to feed myself.

Fortunately for me, therapists aren't there to be dazzled by who we might be; they're there to engage with who we are and who we've been. Keisha isn't nearly as impressed by my BoJack-cribbed monologue about brokenness as she is intrigued that I think of sadness as a birthright. I hadn't realized that other people didn't experience sadness as a thing they felt they deserved.

I make a joke about viewing Good Mental Health as a piece of property; seeing a therapist feels as though I'm renting a couple of Good Days, but I have genetically bad credit that I'll never be able to unspool or overcome. I want her to resolve the Sisyphean task of living, because that's what TV therapists do. She doesn't. She says she understands and asks what my therapy goals are. I don't remember what I said, but I probably launched into a metaphor that took longer than it needed to because I'm uncomfortable with not knowing. I don't remember what I said, but I remember who

I was at twenty-four. I knew there was no cure for the self, and I resented it. I still do.

EXT. Calvary Cemetery

I arrive at my grandmother's grave and there are no fewer than twelve confederate soldiers there. Yes, you read that shit correctly. Calvary Cemetery is a bit of a maze, a low skyline of Irish crosses and roses plucking themselves in the faintest breeze. My father looks up from a conversation we are having—we are coordinating the eulogies we'll be delivering—to point and ask if I'm seeing the same bullshit he's seeing. I confirm that what I see are twelve mothafuckin' confederate soldiers, some with wiry gray beards, others cradling long muskets like children. A moment later we realize they're not here for us, nor are they ghosts come to haul my grandmother's soul away. It might sound ridiculous, but part of being Black is that you're game for any haunting the nation can dream up. It turns out they're confederate war reenactors, performing a faux twenty-one-gun salute over their lost co-worker's grave. Because it's been years all of their faces polish down to nothing, beyond the windows of the car it is both 2020 and 1868. Grief slurs years together, yet while she lived my grandmother never forgot my name once. The guilt of that cements in my stomach as I look out at the silent muskets and the socially distanced confederates. I forget what year it is for a moment, every story about grief is also a story about time and time's arrow neither stands still nor reverses.

What year is it exactly is a question that *BoJack Horseman* as a show gave a tremendous amount of weight to. It's a running question of a mostly solid but at times cluttered first season wherein BoJack meets Diane Nguyen, his ghostwriter, and falls in and out of love with her four or five times before the show settles into the fact they will be friends in the way disagreeable mirrors are often homies. From season two on though, the show was a genre-bending epic, often moving between years and periods when it suited the show. Putting aside that seeing 2007 get its first real treatment as a period piece, and how ridiculously old that made me feel, *BoJack* was a show that understood that grief, depression and anxiety are not born unto us immediately, that these are often matters of a hereditary sadness, a generational trauma that mashes all years together. The show's penultimate episodes routinely get into the kind of Hunter S. Thompson acidic flow that peaks with "Time's Arrow," an episode that surrounds an elderly Beatrice Horseman with a small battalion of faceless maids in 1960s outfits as her aging mind struggles to separate history from the present.

I was in my grandmother's life the shortest of anyone she could still remember. She never was lucid enough to ask me, "What are you doing in Mississippi?" and I never was old enough to tell her I came looking for a long history of disappearing. When she was most biting towards my father, I resented that she remembered to be kind to me but not the boy she raised. Not the child she locked outside when racist children chased him home from school so that he would learn what she knew: the world is fight or sink and nothing else. I didn't know how to hold that fear, that one day her same fever could pull my father under. That the people I love most, myself included, could one day forget me but still walk the earth. What's a ghost in the face of that, what's twelve ghosts when you have generations to choose from?

INT. Therapist's Office

One of the administrators at the counseling center tells me that "Miss Keisha is no longer with us." This does not mean, like I assumed, that Miss Keisha is dead. It means over the summer she got a better job at a counseling center that doesn't limit students to ten sessions per calendar year whether they're stressed about exams or looking for reasons to stay alive.

Later that semester I'm talking to my new therapist, Daniel, about pain and utility. He asks what I mean and I point to my knees. The injuries that've slowly eroded my will to live, that make it difficult to stand in line in excess of ten minutes and have kept me mostly wincing and earthbound since I was sixteen. I tell him they didn't happen at a high school football game like most people presume. I fell off a basketball rim I grabbed during a vertical competition among the homies. To me this is bad damage that was mostly meaningless, pain that I deserve because it was my fault I got hurt, pain I can't turn into anything else. Then I point to my hip and describe the feeling of someone slowly dragging a tiny scalpel over the torn part like a bow, how when I walk the pain is the world's smallest violin. That injury actually did happen in a football game; a boy in yellow and black, whose eyes I can still see and number I can still rehearse (55), yammed down on my shoulders and I curled up on the ground. I was shuffled off the field, limped around for a few minutes, then lied so I could get back in the game. After my coach believed my lie, with what would later be revealed as a small tear in my hip/groin, I played the rest of the game on offense and defense making more tackles than I ever made when I still had two good legs. I tell him I didn't know that was the last day I'd ever have two good legs, just that I knew that I'm a part of something and that's good enough for me.

Daniel doesn't see much difference between the two injuries, to him both pains come from equally meaningless sources. He's not wrong, but I don't want him to be right so I double down on how there's Good Damage that can be made into something else and Bad Damage that, to quote myself, "doesn't advance the plot at all."

There's a moment towards the end of the episode "Good Damage" that conveys it better than I ever did to Daniel. Diane, freshly spiraling over the fact her collection of essays is going nowhere, despairs flatly to Princess Carolyn that she doesn't want all of her pain to have been for nothing. That every moment that she has felt alone, she assumed that to be the bearer of that much pain, to nurse it in your mind, must be because she was being pushed towards making something special. She believed, as I believed, that the pain can tell us that we're special. I believed for many years that the decision to go back into the game despite my hip holding together by a thread is a story about my character as much as Diane on-screen believes that her writer's block is a consequence of hers. I believed this was what Diane calls Good Damage, the kind that allows Kintsugi bowls to become small constellations where once they were merely fractured. I would tell the story of how I'd torn my hip and feel every fractured moment of pain filling with gold. I thought the damage made me who I was, and since I couldn't undo the pain—I wore it. I thought that in taking the pleasure of trying to dunk, of going just a bit too high and coming down not knowing that I would never walk the same again was Bad Damage, was a deserved consequence for my vanity in doing something I loved simply because I loved it. But all that shit was just a younger version of me trying to rationalize what was beyond my control.

Realistically, there was no good or bad damage, there was only ever me and the world I'd mostly survived. The trauma and damage I'd undergone was more like the time eleven years after a stray basketball jammed my right pinky finger, I learned it had actually been fractured with the bone healing at a slight angle, a palm tree bowing to a long-past storm just like most of my lower body. I don't know how to say to Daniel that I both want and dread a therapist looking at me with the disbelief of my doctor when I said I hadn't "noticed" the fracture. That I want him to find the things that have changed the direction of my body without my notice. But that I'm also afraid to release this idea. That to look truly at the damage I've endured is to acknowledge that I'm likely full of fractures I have doused in fool's gold. Pain that is for something is inevitably still pain; no matter how much loyalty you show a wound, it isn't all of what makes you who you are. Pain don't make you good, but I wanted to be good, I wanted to be good more than I wanted to be alive.

EXT. Calvary Cemetery

My father called days before the funeral as we were waiting with the news that Grandma had entered a coma and that it was extremely unlikely that she would ever wake from it. I hadn't taken it seriously, not because I was in denial but simply because I'd thought she was too mean to be killed by anything in this world. The previous century asked my grandmother to be tougher than a human being should have to be to do normal human being things, and since the turn of that century here's an incomplete list of shit she survived:

A quadruple bypass surgery executed in 2005. After the surgery was complete, the doctor confided to my father that Dorothy Mae Leland Randall had perhaps a year left on this earth.

Five years, if fate was feeling kind.

Eight years later, she slipped and fell, cracking her hip, after which she could no longer live alone.

Fifteen years after the quadruple bypass, she contracted COVID, pre-vaccine, over the age of ninety, in an assisted living facility.

She beat it in two weeks.

So, when my father called and said, "Well, buddy, it's happened," I knew what he meant and still, it seemed unimaginable. He tried to convince me that I didn't need to come to the funeral, that he would be fine on his own; in many ways he had been preparing for this moment all his life. But I knew he would want someone with him; a couple of days later we are outside in the grass of the cemetery as I deliver a eulogy that I had often thought of giving but never written down.

Whenever I imagined giving my grandmother's eulogy, it was always inside a church of deep oak, the buttered light pouring on down through yellowing stained glass. Instead, over the heads of the mourners I see a stray confederate soldier wandering between the graves, less a ghost than a sight gag. I'm looking at the mourners, most of whom I barely know, and tell stories of my grandmother that make me feel that we may have come to bury different people. I think of the "Free Churro" episode of *BoJack* and tell the assembled that I will miss that my grandmother was the only one who called me "baby." That I will miss the way I could hear my name bloom in her mouth, one syllable at a time. How it opened in the thin gold hours, when she could remember who I was, she said my name like a morning glory. In my daydreams of what I would say for my grandmother, who didn't own any furniture without a layer of plastic on it, I would finally make sense of all the different women I'd seen her be in my brief life. In later years, I imagined it told a story of where she'd been and who it had made her. But instead, I'd spent the moments before hearing of Aunt Dot, a woman of sharp wit and a towering laugh, who quoted baseball statistics and let young nieces braid her hair as a treat. My grandmother was

lying dead, inches from me in a casket the same uninterrupted blue of Greenville's sky in June. My grandmother was
lying dead, and I was ashamed—too ashamed to admit this
was perhaps the closest I'd ever felt to her.

The fifth-season *BoJack Horseman* episode "Free
Churro" is perhaps the series at the height of its powers.
A single, nearly uninterrupted monologue from BoJack on
the occasion of his mother's funeral. It's an episode that one
can watch without much context and find some small pocket
of grief warm enough to burrow inside. I spent much of a
summer watching and rewatching it, knowing that one day
my father would give a eulogy for his mother, and wondering
what could be said.

Just as the episode is approaching its volta, BoJack says
that losing a parent is a bit like *Becker*, the one show that
even Ted Danson couldn't all the way save. BoJack says that
Becker had all the right pieces to be a legendary show: great
writers, a talented cast, interesting characters, but despite
all those good pieces, they could never put it together. That
you could spend the length of *Becker* waiting for it to get better, but like the relationship between Beatrice and BoJack,
between Dorothy and James, that one day it would all be over
and it would never have a chance to improve. It's not profound
to say death is permanent for the dead. But there it was.
That one day my father, my first favorite writer, would open
his mouth to say that the woman who raised him, harmed
him, birthed him, hugged him, was gone. The woman whose
back room he lived in with my infant sister. The back room
he sprinted out of after someone threw a brick through the

window so that he could catch the man and throw him not into, and not over, but directly on top of a chain-link fence.

I am telling you about watching my father, his pale-blue mask curled in his palm, tell the few mourners who could gather about his mother, of a woman who never again would be able to look at him from across a room and say that she sees him. He doesn't mention that the last time he had come to see her he had heard her say, "I don't want to talk to that nigga, his daddy liked him better anyway." Instead, he made jokes, he entertained the way he always had. My father moved his hands in ecstatic impressions of his mother and rolls of chuckles came from our cousins, and for a moment I saw his grin pull at the edge of his mouth before watching his shoulders sink just slightly, the gravity of where we were standing washing briefly back over him. Because he knew that my grandmother was a hard Black woman from a hard place who lived a life that was often relentlessly difficult, he played the good son and steeled his shoulders and went back to trying to make people laugh. He knew that she loved for him to make people laugh, and that, if nothing else, he could try again one last time to make her happy. He could be her son, one last time.

INT. Therapist's Office

I tell my newest therapist, Jason, that progress has stopped feeling like progress, then watch his waves glimmer in the track lighting of his office as his brow creases. He asks me what exactly I want to progress towards and I start telling him a story about Princess Carolyn, BoJack's high-strung agent and a Virgo icon. Jason's never seen many of the shows that I use as shorthand when he's asking me a question that requires me to describe, or even worse just *feel*, an emotion I can't explain. But you know this trick; I'm doing a version of it with you now.

In the final episode of *BoJack Horseman*, "Nice While It Lasted," BoJack is attending Princess Carolyn's wedding. He has been granted furlough from a prison stint for breaking into his old house and nearly drowning in the pool. Princess Carolyn and BoJack share a dance, and I know it's Amy Sedaris voicing her but I hear me when she tells him, "I guess I'm afraid of losing a part of myself. I'm afraid that if I let someone else take care of me, then I'm not really me anymore. I'm afraid of getting too comfortable, going soft. I'm afraid this could be the best thing that ever happened to me, and if it doesn't make me as happy as it's supposed to, then I'm a lost cause."

Jason nods and lets me keep unspooling the story, which I appreciate. But eventually, the dude has to do his job and he asks me again what I feel I'm progressing towards. I shrug. I know what I want, but to say it makes it feel somehow irretrievable. I want to believe that my life is pulling towards some ending that is both surprising and inevitable. I want to admit that more often than not, I'm exhausted. And there is no progress that won't leave me feeling exhausted unless I'm willing to accept allowing someone to take care of me. Progress used to feel like I was coming back to life, now each step forward feels like a reminder the life I built is unsustainable. But I don't know how to reach out that hand, how to accept that the lack of support in my worst years doesn't unmake the abundance of my beloveds' hands reaching out to try and hold me gently now. I sprinted out of the first therapist's office I set foot in and at times I'm so short of breath I wonder if I have been running ever since.

Jason thumbs his beard and asks if I think that sometimes I mistake destination for healing, or maybe he only asks that in my head, but either way I let the silence fill the room, because what else is there?

I've been guilty of living my mental health journey with the hope there's an "other side." What I wanted was an ending, a door to walk through and instead, I'm still just me. There is perhaps no "other side," only my mind going through what it feels like it has to go through in the same way the melting-clock logic of *BoJack*'s penultimate episode, "The View from Halfway Down," finds BoJack at a dinner table with every loved one he's had who has died. Everyone has gathered to do one last talent show, including his mother, Beatrice. The scenes are meant to stretch and bend credulity, to make us ask whether BoJack is in purgatory or a dream. And they do succeed in that, but I found a sense of wonder as well. That this is the last time we ever see Beatrice Horseman, and it is a swan song fitting of one of BoJack's only lasting relationships. Beatrice's performance comes last, a solo dance to her brother's favorite song, her ribbon trailing behind her as if she means to leash the moon. Just before she launches herself up into the sky, she assures BoJack that this is the hard part before the easy part, passing through the doorframe onstage, the ribbon first cocooning her then unraveling in shadow over BoJack's face where once there was a mother and now there is only light.

The last time I saw my grandmother, her face was upside down as the mortician showed my father a picture of how she had looked in her closed casket. Her hair was long, braided into a small cord that rested over her shoulder, her dress a cerulean fit for the place between stars. And so my grandmother passed from this world, in a blue dress and blue casket, a handful of miles from where her father's running had stopped. I can't explain why, but whenever I imagine that day she left Greenville behind forever, there's not a cloud in sight, the weather never varies, everything above her pudgy outstretched hand is a humming periwinkle the shade of her casket. And so this is how my grandmother passed from this world—at the end of her pain, she became the sky.

There's an argument to be made that the entire final episode takes place in BoJack's head, that in reality he did drown in his own pool, that he was never meant to survive. But I want BoJack to have survived because that means the show did what it did best right to the very end—refuse resolution. BoJack must live with the people he's harmed, the relationships that have outgrown him, and also his own potential to put more good into the world. Just like any of us, really. Sometimes, the great cruelty and wonder of life is as simple as the fact that it continues, even when we have romanced too often the view from halfway down. Like anyone, I have my depressed days where I am merely looking for someone to sit a spell with me as the waters rush in. But more and more, I've been thinking about what it is to arrive at letting someone else take care of you after a whole life dreading needing care from anyone. I've been letting myself need more often, to say what I need into the isolation of the dark and find one of my beloveds' hands reach to catch me. Once I was a boy whose life and memory was disintegrating to jump cuts, once I was a boy who ran out of the first therapist's office he ever saw. I am still him, somedays. This isn't about perfection, it's about being as persistent in my healing as I have been in my grief.

The final shot of *BoJack Horseman* is the same as the first shot of "Nice While It Lasted," BoJack and Diane atop a roof in the open air, the navy gradient of the sky expanding endlessly above them as they try to map the space between each other without speaking. Each is dressed blue as my grandmother in her casket, blue as a forgiveness that now can never come.

The BETTER ANGELS of AARON SORKIN

The mystic chords of memory will swell when again touched, as surely they will be, by the better angels of our nature.

— Abraham Lincoln, first inaugural address, 1861

Never mind that no kingdom was ever won by small gestures.

— Carl Phillips, "No Kingdom"

When my name was called for the American Legion Patriotism Award, I assumed it was a joke—even though I knew I deserved to win. Actually, I never heard my name; just the applause. I am seventeen in the chapel of my high school, sitting in the row reserved for seniors. I am sitting in a pew near the front where I can occasionally lean back and take in the stained glass of the window. The first signs of spring in Minnesota sunlight sliding weary through the stain. In the pew with me are all the Black boys in my grade, all four of us sit where nobody can tell if we're singing along or not. We are here with the same expectation as every year: we are here to watch, to listen, and to never hear our names.

School awards day was boring as hell if you weren't expecting to win anything. The four of us weren't supposed to sit together since we were never in the same advisory. Still, anywhere we went we had our rituals. On awards day we'd quietly run our fingers down the program, thumbing each award and shaking our heads occasionally like we were reviewing bad trailers in a movie theater. We didn't win anything sophomore year, or junior year, which was cool since we typically didn't like the kind of kids who won. We all had relatively easy names to say, but most of the kids who won awards had very easy names to have.

So when the head of school called my name that day, I wasn't listening for myself. The homies turned and asked why I wasn't moving, getting closer to the little gold medal nestled against black velvet. The homies lifted me up and thrust me into the row between the pews to walk softly towards the stage and all the grinning faces.

I was sure it was a prank, this award had been earmarked for another boy in my class for years. He won half the history awards every year, came to school in an American flag vest the day Bin Laden was killed, and spoke in inflated sentences on gun rights and all the ways this country we both wanted to run someday was rusting the further it got from its origins. He was not the first person in his family to have his exact name, he talked about it—a lot. What must it be like to have an heirloom that easy? But somehow the award was mine and I was for many years a dedicated patriot of the lie of America—some days, in spite of myself, I miss it.

Aaron Sorkin's *The West Wing* is, in many ways, a perfection of that lie. It's a fantasy held among liberals that America was once a country governed by the ideas of very smart (read: white) people and that the country can be great again, when its governance is returned to those Very Smart People. But while *The West Wing*—its rapid-fire banter and tracking shots—is popularly considered Sorkin's masterpiece, I think he's never come closer to being honest about the failings of his politics than in the first ten minutes of his much less successful HBO series, *The Newsroom*.

The Newsroom was a show that never outgrew its first scene. Sorkin's point man and protagonist, Will McAvoy, waxes poetic for roughly five minutes on the fact that there is no statistical evidence to suggest America is the greatest country in the world. "We're seventh in literacy, twenty-seventh in math, twenty-second in science, forty-ninth in life expectancy, a hundred and seventy-eighth in infant mortality, third in median household income, number four in labor force and number four in exports. We lead the world in only three categories: number of incarcerated citizens per capita, number of adults who believe angels are real, and defense spending, where we spend more than the next twenty-six countries combined, twenty-five of whom are allies." It comes close but Sorkin's America needs to believe there is a "we" in America. "It sure used to be . . . We stood up for what was right. We fought for moral reason. We passed laws, struck down laws, for moral reason. We waged wars on poverty, not on poor people. We sacrificed, we cared about our neighbors, we put our money where our mouths were and we never beat our chest." Despite being born here, I wanted very badly to be an American. I knew nothing else and imagination can be brutal for the stateless. I could no longer maintain my mostly theoretical citizenship in this "we."

Before I saw *The Newsroom* scene, I heard it. A fellow Black boy and once dear friend who loved politics read it to me aloud between long pulls from a blunt. The words fell between the smoke. Listening to him, I built an entire country within this America. This America, which reminded us every day and especially the year I finally graduated college, that it had never been the greatest country for us.

It's become common to say that the 2016 election was not surprising. I've said it too. Both because I believe it and because I was raised to never underestimate what white folks are capable of. Some white folk spent the next few days loud in their confusion over what they had done. And it pissed me off, to watch people perform innocence in a house that had been burning for a long time. I wanted to be unsurprised. I wanted to be unfeeling. But the unsayable thing is that on that night, I lost some understanding of what governs white people.

I had fallen in love as a teenager with the false idea that what governs white people is written down somewhere, legible and systemic. And in my arrogance I genuinely thought

I'd understood it intricately for years. That American lie is that this country has systems in place to prevent such a deep mutilation. I've often joked that electoral math is the only math I've ever known, ever loved. Of course, what is rarely discussed on *The West Wing* is that that math, around which most of the characters' lives revolve, is inherently predicated on racist ideology. That math is the primary reason I would once have been counted as three-fifths of a person. This is the only argument I need for why electoral math can't protect anyone. It was a bad nostalgia to bend to, one at the heart of what parts of me still lived in Aaron Sorkin's America.

I was trying, I think, to protect myself against the true lawlessness of a white imagination. An imagination that is willing to ignore extraordinary violence so that America might be returned to a place of moral authority and prosperity it has never seen. I knew before Trump was elected that the country could not be saved by small gestures, by lies, by nostalgia, by incremental tolerances that we call progress when it suits us, by an unearned "we."

I left that night the citizen only of a hard truth, that the country cannot be saved.

Patriotism requires some investment in forgetting. I come from people with good reason to remember what others want to forget. Consider that one of *The West Wing*'s most prominent Black characters, Charlie Young, only existed after something was "forgotten." Charlie was brought on in the third episode only after the NAACP complained about the implications of the show's all-white main cast. Charlie was meant to serve as our representation; a little nod from the show that for so many years we watched from where we were, without ever hearing our names. Here's another thing rarely spoken of. Charlie appeared in original drafts of *The West Wing*'s pilot but was apparently phased out as it took its final form. It feels so familiar to learn this is maybe one of Charlie's Blackest traits, that he was in the original text and still was almost lost by the patriots of forgetting.

As I first wrote this I was on the run from another forgetting. In Oxford, white supremacist protestors marched in torrential rain from one confederate monument to another. All off a rumor that, after all this time, the statues may come down. I fled the town I live in, out of the place I pay rent for, precisely because men with open carry permits and guns, women with MAGA hats and signs, pulled up to make clear what they will do to defend their forgetting. They are patriots of a kind. Patriots who have convinced themselves that they owe allegiance not just to this country that loves them enough to kill me, but to a Zero Country none of them have ever seen or lived in. They have brought their children, who will also wear red hats. I imagine this is how their parents are teaching them, one march at a time, the terrible urgency of hearing your name.

In the Mississippi town where I lived they sold red hats that say "Make America Read Again." There are many people who buy those hats, who think this is funny; I do not. This is not the only place in the world that sells such hats, there's an epidemic of parodies. "Make America Gay Again," "Make America Smart Again." And on and on as if America needed a reminder of its relationship with the word "again."

Maybe you have what I have, and have an elder to ask what you're doing down in Mississippi and understands what you mean when you tell them you're searching for what happens to the body when the hustle goes bad. Maybe you too have an elder who can look at our dissolving world and say, "Once they had knives." "Once they bombed our house, our whole block, and nobody is allowed to remember." "Once we couldn't come here at all." "Once our name was _____ and maybe someday you can make it that again."

The living white supremacists, patriots of forgetting, want to remind and return to a theoretical time when this country was great, though I could not have written this to you then. The living liberals want to remind and return us to a time when the country was run nearly exclusively by "incredibly intelligent" people who considered me subhuman and legislated accordingly. The dead need no reminding that these visions are predicated on the subjection of Black, indigenous, queer, poor, trans, disabled, POC. From a distance, the red hats look the same, are the same. I don't know what the hat says, but I know it makes me think you stormed the Capitol. I know it means you have an investment in forgetting. I know it means you are more American than me.

I know that Nostalgia is heavily armed on both sides.

I say that sometimes I miss being a patriot of Sorkin's version of the American lie. For what I imagine are the same reasons Baldwin wrote, "To be a negro in this country and be relatively conscious is to be in a rage almost all the time" and also "I love America more than any other country in this world, and, exactly for this reason, I insist on the right to criticize her perpetually" in the course of the same brilliant life. Once I began to remove myself from a national lie I became a certain kind of stateless. It is brutal and lonely out here tending to the past.

The last word ever spoken on *The West Wing* is quiet against the theme song seeping like the sun through the window of *Air Force One*. The last word is "tomorrow," as in "Tomorrow you can love me and the ones I love, or you can love your nostalgia, but you can't love both." I confess, I missed the word "tomorrow" the first time I watched the finale. I had to rewind the DVD, or maybe even then my own patriotism was crumbling.

AGAINST GRACE

For those of y'all who don't remember or chose to forget, there is a video of an ash-haired President Barack Obama singing "Amazing Grace" in a church in South Carolina. Everyone behind him is Black and draped in long church robes, deep & purple as elegies. It is the summer and everything is slick. It is the summer and a toll must be paid. From my room in Philly the Wi-Fi is shaky, everyone behind Obama is a tulip or a bruise depending on the lag. There is a funeral going on that seems to have been going on all year. Obama opens his mouth, he says a new version of what we always say about goodness, about possibility. Nobody says the word "assassination," nobody says "betrayal," everyone sings along. The song stutters in and nobody says "forgiveness," but it's implied and encouraged. I sink and sweat into the mattress. I look at the window and think about mercy. I leave the clip on a loop and all along the internet folks say it is one of the best speeches of Obama's presidency. I rise to get a glass of water I've been thinking about for over an hour and I can see the outline of myself on the bed. It is June, I can see myself evaporating.

More unites Black people than song, and less unites Black people than non-Black people seem compelled to believe. I'm related to zero percent of the Black people I've been asked if I'm related to. I don't know people's co-workers or that "guy that used to date my cousin." I know very few people, actually. What does unite every Black person I've ever known, though, is being compelled to thank or forgive white people for something that, were the roles reversed, they would have killed us for. Silence is not always silent. Grace is not always silent. Sometimes it is a tooth falling into a palm, and that palm never curling into a fist.

Once, I was in the process of losing a tooth. For weeks that canine hung by a thread from my small body. I was seven and a white boy I went to school with was seven. Before this, fights were a sound we made with our mouths. We always won and never bled.

When he punched me the little tether snapped and my mouth tasted like copper and then tasted like a mouth again. I caught the tooth, I didn't swing back, I feigned thanks to him. This is maybe the oldest thing I have ever remembered: the moment when I knew I could win the fight but that I would lose in some larger way. I told my family what happened. I told them it was an accident and maybe even believed it. I reached for the religion of believing in the best of people who put blood in my mouth. I placed the tooth beneath my pillow and in the morning there were two faded dollar bills, pulpy and soft like feathers.

In the two most famous clips I know of, Obama has a tendency to start singing before he starts singing. He is measured, graceful, hyper aware of what his voice can and cannot reasonably pull off. He doesn't belt out notes, he kinda slowly two-steps his way into them like an uncle wading into a soul train line. In the clip of him at the Charleston funeral he's shaking his head, a mightcouldbe under his tongue, as he says "grace" over and over again, like it's pulling him towards something. The whole thing seems almost spontaneous, and who am I to say it wasn't? Those first notes come out flat if we're being honest, but hell, maybe the song is tired too.

Grace is less about healing than it is about manageable pain.

The story of "Amazing Grace" has been told out of order so many times that the bones of the song healed crooked. Part of the myth is true: John Newton did write "Amazing Grace" after having been the captain of a slave ship. The ship passed through a storm that threatened to drown him, and he did eventually become an abolitionist. He stayed in the slave trade for another five years after finding religion— convenient. He wrote the song roughly twenty-four years after the storm, for him, had passed—convenient. In the version that me and some of my homies grew up with, Newton wrote the song with the storm still rolling over him. Epiphany is funny like that, it can be made to look spontaneous even with the dead lying at one's feet.

The summer of 2015 was belligerently hot and death made it hotter. I remember what it was like that summer watching Obama call out the names of those assassinated by the coward Dylan Roof, saying they had "found that grace." I remember wondering if this was the fate of Blackness, to be shot by a stranger you prayed over. I remember learning that the cops had brought Roof Burger King. I was too tired to be surprised.

Forgiveness, or something like it, has always been seen as Black people's superpower; whiteness has a parasitic relationship with that forgiveness. I'm done indulging it. I have spent my adulthood trying to pry white folks' wants out of my throat before I am asked to forgive again. I am asked. I try. I fail and fail because sometimes I want to survive. Whiteness cannot sustain its allegiance to moral mediocrity. I wish that wasn't my problem; I deserve for it not to be.

I never doubt the grace of Black people, it is the only reason I am still alive. I would like, though, to divorce grace from what I cannot forgive. I feel compelled to say that one of the great tragedies of whiteness is that one goes to the grave with no clue of how often they've been spared. I have no such luxury. I feel compelled to say that there are no tragedies of whiteness. Tragedy implies a choice was withheld, and whiteness always has a choice and it will always choose the path of my destruction.

In my mind the grace that obliges the unforgivable is always spelled with a lowercase *g*. I don't know if I believe all the way in true freedom anymore. Though it sounds like a destination rather than a constant process, freedom is a thing that takes practice and repetition; you cannot arrive at being free.

But we love destinations in America.

What I need is a practice of freedom that I don't need to preface by saying, "It ain't much but . . ." So that it's not dismissed as conspiracy theory when I name what I have absolutely seen. That last one is proving harder than it sounds, the arm of forgetting is as long as a country, but narrow as a gaze, meager as the imagination of white folks who sit in police cars and statehouses and restaurants and department meetings and classrooms united by their instinct to punish Black folks for living, loving, styling, flexing, imagining and forgiving ourselves, and them too, most if not all of the time.

When they cannot punish us, they punish those we love; when they cannot punish them, and even when they can, they punish themselves.

White supremacy is a death cult, a religion for the feral. I'm tired of epiphany, it's nearly June again, I'm tired of the rain, I'm tired of waiting for it to be God enough.

GRIEF Ft.
KANYE WEST

At the tip of my father's fingers is Kanye West, within his hands is a novel I have never read. I'm twelve and my father is pointing to the screen where the biggest name in 2005 music is dressed like Evel Knievel and getting cussed out by Nia Long. I don't know yet he's finna become my favorite artist or how much it will hurt to love him for a long time before I can't anymore, but I know that I feel what my father describes when he says he heard Prince for the first time on a pirate radio station and fell in love for the third time in his life. Not long after my grandfather died he heard pre-first-album Prince and the smoke he was trying to drown his grief in cleared for just a moment. Prince played all his own instruments, wrote all his own songs, and my father never met another Black boy with that many hands.

I learned all of this the day I saw my father watching *Purple Rain* for the first time and asked him what he was watching. His hand is still big enough to swallow my eight-year-old shoulder and at the end of my father's fingers is Prince in a jacket holding him close as the petals of a salvia as he says, "This boy lost his daddy too, but his daddy showed him the music so now he's playing to show his daddy how much he loves the music." And this is the first elegy that I have ever heard, the moment I realize that maybe grief is meant to be sung. That one day, I will speak at his funeral. I ran up the stairs, grabbed a stringless guitar and sat in his lap so I could hear the rest of "Purple Rain." Feeling his tears falling behind me sometimes feels like the closest I have ever gotten to reading the novel he hasn't finished since grief altered the course of his life forever. In all my memories of this day the sun is already pulling low along my block, a tiny me watching my dad, my first favorite artist, watch his favorite artist and wonder who will sing to me when he's gone.

It may read like metaphor, but November 10, 2007, really did bloom over Chicago a dry, gray 34 degrees. The weather in Chicago makes many drafts of grief, this is the story of one of them. So November 10 found me, a high school freshman, carrying two backpacks off the 151 bus. Only one of those bags had books in it.

Inside a ratty blue-gray polyester backpack was a pair of pristine black-and-white Timbs. The coldest winter of Kanye West's life had only begun, in some ways we have this in common.

Whatever has or needs to be said about Kanye West at the time this arrives to you, there is one thing upon which we can all agree: that Kanye loved his mother, Donda. Her dying day which, as it turned out, was the day that I donned a light brown Rocawear jean suit my father found on clearance at J.C. Penney. That summer it was too hot to wear anything that didn't drape. And part of a flex is that you never put yourself in a position to sweat in some shit you can't replace. And if you can't avoid sweat, you better make folk believe it's because you're the summer itself.

The ninth-grade hallway in my school sat at the top of three flights of stairs. Every day I arrived with my half-broken headphones blasting "Touch the Sky." November 10, 2007, I was swapping out my snow-soaked G-Unit sneakers for my Timbs at the bottom of a stairwell when someone above was the first to mention that Donda West died.

Later that day, sitting with two white boy homies of mine all I could think was that Donda West was dead. I didn't know how beloved she was at Chicago State, the hundreds of students she had mentored and inspired. What I knew was that less than two months after *Graduation* dropped, Kanye's mother was gone. I felt the loneliness of a man I would never know, a stranger's grief branching in my chest. All because he once made me feel like a depressed Black boy from Chicago was the most legible thing in the world.

The white boy homies, for their part, were sad. And minutes later were joking that Kanye was likely headed to the studio the minute that the funeral was over. With this loss, the next album would be fire.

In that moment, almost passable as a true joke, I glimpsed what I thought was another electric angle on grief. The dead in my house most often meant my father's father. All my life, my father had struggled under the weight of everything he never wrote to his own father. It slouched him, he wore grief like an anvil. He still does. I had never read the novel my father has been writing all my life, I wasn't old enough to doubt it would ever come. I knew that my father had been trying to master the pain of being cut off from his art by his own grief, I knew he was afraid that one day his death would be a surprise that suffocated all of my art. I knew but couldn't say that my father's greatest fear was that I am just like him. I knew but couldn't say it was becoming my greatest fear too. But Kanye could make an old song whine faster and higher until it was everybody's ancestor. I figure maybe this is what everyone who "misses the old Kanye" has meant. Through the sample, Kanye somehow defied death. In Kanye's hands the dead owned no past tense.

It's some white nonsense to believe anyone can grow into a better artist by losing the person who made living worth it. Still, we expect this of artists all the time. As non-white as I am, I too fuck up like this sometimes. Believing that there is a way to make grief productive—that grief ought to be productive.

I figured that if Kanye could make this album, perfect as my father's unfinished novel, forge some classic from insurmountable grief, then maybe sadness was less of a feeling than an industry. Forgive me, I liked that idea more than my own softness. I come from an industrial place; I liked the idea that I could be more than human, industrial with grief; electric in the worst of melody. I don't know what

Kanye wanted, not that day and definitely not now. Not the man whose combination of fame, a neurodegenerative condition he refuses to care for consistently, and straight-up anti-Semitism is currently on television putting forth unforgivable lies and conspiracy theories about Jewish people in a world where, to quote Yaron Weitzman, "Conspiracy theories about Jewish people lead to dead Jewish people."

In the years before I know this, before *this* is Kanye West—I like to imagine.

And a younger me imagined that maybe Kanye wanted industry too, maybe Kanye wanted some assurance that grief could be controlled and isn't just a weather that arrives when it pleases. Perhaps, seeing nothing left to trust, he turned to his own hands. A better freedom, we rationalized, like boys do, to grind. Grind until you forget you carry the need to be useful.

I carry the need to be useful. I grieve like this, almost always. I suppress each new sadness then wait for whatever small and needful spark in my brain can taunt them into pitchy harmony. This is my industry, and like my body, I'm never confident on how to turn it off. I'm like Kanye this way and maybe only this way. Forgive me, I thought I owed it; it has been a decade and more, I've still never found out to who.

�꒰

A LITTLE OVER a year later, *808's & Heartbreak* debuted in a Chicago besieged by another gray and relentless 34 degrees.

808's is most famous in the Kanye canon for its use of auto-tune, Kanye's voice is already on its way to becoming un-recognizable. The album is often claustrophobic and warbly, like a speaker left too long in the rain. The album was a jar-ring leap dropping soaring horns for an artillery of bucking drums. The sped-up soul samples that were Kanye's signa-ture were gone. *808's* is quiet by comparison, unsettlingly still. I like to imagine that if me and Kanye were friends, I'd have been concerned. We ain't friends, so I just bobbed my head where the beat found me.

Every feature on *808's* sounds like the smile I use to tell the homies I'm OK when we both know I'm lying.

Maybe that's on me, for trying to make space inside my own grief, reaching back to who I know I can never be again. During "Amazing" Jeezy grimly chuckles as a form of punc-tuation. The lead singles off of *808's*, first "Love Lockdown" and then "Heartless," both try to strike a balance between a private grief and public demand. Either the moral of both songs is that the only way out is through or the moral of both is that there is no way out.

But what I loved about *808's*, and still do, is that it feels like in a lifetime built from trusting what could be made from the voices of others, that it is the first time Kanye trusts his own voice. Sure, it's always been clear that Kanye loves the sound of his own voice. But in *808's* voice is more than instrument, it's a morose city Kanye reaches a hand out from and a decade later I do not know if the hand means:

This is my only country now, I would like to show it to you. Please, respect the weather.

Or

This is my only country now, once I had a mother and now my allegiance is to nowhere. This is the anthem of where I live. To you it may only sound like static.

On "Street Lights" Kanye's grief-stricken voice emerges from a distorted siren, riding a wave of static asking if he still has time to grow. The song is a single lyric that repeats in fragments, it fades and the echo told a teenage me an old story. A story about begging forgiveness from what cannot answer you.

Sophomore year of high school I listened to "Street Lights" on the bus ride home from basketball games. My jersey extra starchy beneath my armpits as I lay on my back, trying to push myself below the noise and further into the dark. Kanye used auto-tune almost as second-person narration, a way to say every grief but dress it in a "you." I'm guilty of doing the same with you, reader. I know that one day, I will say my father's name when he is dead and my voice will be unadorned; mine. Maybe it is impossible for bois like us to make good on a song about the irreversible if we can recognize ourselves in the process.

There are 66,000 views on a video of me fucking up. Or the third thing that comes up when you search for my name is a video of me convincing an audience full of people that I am not fucking up. In the video I'm twenty-one years old, doing a poem called "Grief" because I didn't know what else to name it. For many people, maybe thousands, this three minutes is as old as I will ever be and as much as they'll ever remember me having said. And still, I fucked up.

Wearing a "Silence Will Not Save You" T-shirt, I'm doing a poem that, at the time, was the best thing I'd ever written. It's about my recurring dreams of being shot by a police officer, it's the kind of poem where I say "body" again and again, the syllables thudding at my feet like hail. It's my last college poetry slam ever. I do this poem three to five times a week. I clock into grief like a job. I'm young enough to think I can be in this kind of pain professionally; I'm a young enough artist that this kind of meticulously edited and sharply choreographed pain is all I can think to want.

Two days later, I'll win the Best Poet Award and feel like this is the beginning of everything turning around. I'll hope that the time I spent reading poems about Black people who were murdered by a state, which only regretted not murdering them faster, will inspire that state not to do the lone thing it was designed to do. I will be wrong. I will have unrealistic expectations about what Black art can do to stop bullets. I will have unrealistic expectations about what Black art can do to save me.

I will refuse to save me.

In a week, I'll receive an email telling me I'm not graduating with my class. There will be an identical letter in my mailbox because cruelty sometimes dresses up as thoroughness. I will go to my niggas quietly, one by one, to tell them that I am disappointed, but I'm fine. None of my niggas who matter will believe me.

But the thing about slam is that it was always about the moment, it was always about the second before the silence breaks. And on video before all of this can happen, my eyes are wrenched shut, reaching for a memory of my college dorm window. Often it was the last thing I saw before I passed out from another autoplay video of Black death. It is 2015, I am proudest of the fact that I'm trained to reach for what hurts, then make it sing. That was the bad miracle, I always knew how to make it sing.

I'm thinking of that singing while I'm watching a twenty-five-year-old Kanye West humming an aimless harmony as his dentist pries the bloodied wires from his gums. Well, I'm thinking of that and I'm thinking of a story about my dad picking up some Chinese food for my mom. Story goes that in the eighties when my parents were living together in New York, my father got his dress shoe stuck in a sewer grate. He felt some shit pop and, as a nigga who had broken many a bone in his life, instantly knew that his foot was broken. Now, a normal person would have tried to go to perhaps . . . a hospital. Maybe a nearby clinic. A fuckin Starbucks at the very least. Instead, this man, my father, looked up the small hill that my mother's favorite Chinese food restaurant sat at the top of, gripped his briefcase tightly and hopped up the hill on his good leg. He ordered on one leg. He hopped back down on one leg. He hailed a cab, still on that same leg, wonton soup and shit casually in hand, hopped into his building and out the elevator down the hall to hand my mother the Chinese food and only then summoned the audacity to say, "Josephine, I think I broke my foot."

When my mother, horrified by her husband using his left leg as a pogo stick for an hour, asked why he was at the apartment, he blinked twice in genuine confusion. "Because you said you wanted Chinese."

I guess what I'm saying is that where I come from, pain isn't an excuse for stopping the work you have to do, especially if that work is on behalf of someone you love, that it is a song you sing even when no music was required or requested.

The fuckup in the most famous video of me starts about two thirds of the way through; nobody notices. Well, nobody notices aside from my team who have been hearing me rehearse this triggering poem repeatedly for hours, for months because I'm determined to get it perfect. I'm determined to make something of the pain, and I did—I made more pain.

The line, one of the poem's emotional climaxes, "Someone, somewhere doesn't know my name but already wants to change the subject," comes out reversed because I've fucked up by fucking myself up. I'm starting to have a panic attack onstage, the aperture of my throat narrowing because everything has a limit and my body is well past that limit. I've been triggering myself to make a living, a living that wasn't even a living just a fancy way to drag my life behind me.

Of course, nobody noticed the fuckup, I hid it well because that was what I did best, can still do best. I landed the end of the poem breathless, my skin sallow, beard ragged and stunted in patches. This is an image of a boi who needed a therapist much more than he needed a microphone, but trusted the microphone infinitely more. I wanted art to be my therapy because I wanted my healing to be a thing I could control. I told you, I wanted to make the hurt sing.

In the second episode of the Netflix documentary *Jeen-yuhs: A Kanye Trilogy* the director, Coodie, who's been film-ing Kanye on and off since he was nineteen, tells a story about the days after Kanye's infamous near fatal car crash. How with a jaw broken in three places, Coodie feared his friend and confidant may never rap again. Instead, Kanye, swollen beyond recognition, called from his hospital bed and rapped the beginnings of what would become "Through the Wire." Much of the legend of Kanye's work ethic begins here, with the story of a boy emerging from twisted metal crowning him-self a rusty winged angel. Maybe this is when it became an expectation that each pain become a classic kind of grief. And it is partially this expectation that allows Kanye to act like an abuser, to shove away anyone and anything that reminds him how he is inflicting his own pain on the people who love him. That reminds him that nothing that loves you wants to watch you work yourself to death. That there is a difference between people who love you and people who are impressed by you. It's a truth you can make a lot of money pretending not to hear.

Let's say what's real, I've chosen being impressive over being loved. In a language and a year where I was dead by the end of most sentences, 2015 me wanted to make some-thing beautiful and undeniable about that pain. I wanted to be brilliant and use that brilliance to provoke white folk to be ashamed of killing me. Slam gave me a family of other artists who loved me and loved what I made. It also gave me a growing platform to ignore that family pleading with me to slow down. My grief began to wear me the way a funeral flower wears its rain. This performed grief that paid my bills and SEPTA tickets, that took me to colleges where similarly exhausted Black students gave me their school's money to reassure them that I was in pain too, but I could make the pain sing. This grief that bought me Wendy's 4 for $4s to nibble between gigs, that bought the tickets as the muscles in my back curdled in the end row of Megabus after Megabus. I forgot what I was beyond my grief; I forgot that a knife gold with honey is still a knife.

On the cusp of another prophetically hot summer I'm on the wrong side of an argument about cancel culture. I am once again arguing for a fiction that I've come to fear with a man I've come to love, my mentor who has also become my nigga. I'm saying that I'm once again in an argument about Kanye, and this time it's because Kanye is wearing a MAGA hat and saying that slavery sounds like it was a choice. I am once again sitting in Mississippi in hot pursuit of yet more evidence that it was anything but that. Nine times out of ten an argument about Kanye is more heated than you should ever be arguing for a nigga who does not and never again will love you. The other thing to know is that every argument about Kanye is heated because most of them are arguments about what I wish I could undo about myself.

My mentor who has become my nigga is trying to explain to me that my argument, that cancel culture is a corrupting carceral instinct on Black people who have no carceral power to wield, is built on faulty logic. He's right because there is no such thing as cancel culture. There is no punishment, truly, for the crime of abandoning Black women and that is irretrievably what Kanye has done, what he has always done.

I meanwhile am worried that this is the fate of people who try to turn their pain into an instrument.

I'm in the second year of my MFA and my first book is on the verge of coming out in the fall. I love that book, and like most things I love, I have asked too much of it. I have imbued the poems in it with my deep and perennial pains, because I wanted what Kanye wanted with *The College Dropout*, with *My Beautiful Dark Twisted Fantasy*, what he will want with *Donda*, to drown what parts of his life he does not want and call the water "mirror." I counted on *Refuse* to do more than change my life, I wanted a new life entirely. I wanted something that art cannot give, only open the door to us changing for ourselves. But in 2018 I'm growing more and more worried that finishing the project doesn't feel the way I hoped. I woke up and all my pain was still loyal only to me. It still is.

Beyond the window, magnolia and pine and Rowan Oak shake in the breeze over Oxford and somewhere Kanye is off, maybe even at the White House, giving a fuck about none of this. And this is the thing that my nigga is trying, with all the patience his bloodshot eyes can house, to explain to me. The man who once made me feel like the most legible thing in the world is gone. And he may never return, but I cannot survive waiting for my memory of him to return. I stretch my fingers together and try not to think about the writer's block that has been stealing over me time and again this semester. I am weary and despite all the hustle that my life as a writer has demanded of me, I've forgotten that it is not my job to be exhausted—it is my job to write. I don't always know the difference. I have spent what feels like several forevers chasing down the roots of my grief, this sadness my voice wears so well that it is almost my name.

There's no real way to take away the voice of a billionaire. There's no billionaire on the planet who needs help with their voice. Kanye, like me, needs help. Kanye, unlike me, doesn't need my help. I don't know how to help myself, I didn't know how to admit that it feels as though I have given my perfect-bound grief to the world. I have no idea what I am worth to the world without some torment to fling the door wide to. And at twenty-four I need, almost as badly as that twenty-one-year-old slam poet me on the video, to be worth *something*.

There are days in Oxford where the sun streams so thick that the light nearly pools in your palm. It's a day like that, where the world is beautiful but I am not, the morning after this argument when I am drafting a text message.

What I wanted was to say something about how my relationship with Kanye is almost always parallel to my relationship with forgiveness. That I believe at some core level that my pains are my fault, my griefs are my fuel. I was wrong, I was wrong about all of it. I was forgiveless with that wrongness, merciless with myself as I dreamed I could gild my failures. I took the wound, I took another, I wrote them down and watched myself wrench each cut open like a door—then smiled at the sound it made.

What I wrote in the text to my mentor was something like this:

Hey my g, thanks for that talk last night, I'm sorry my voice got hot. I'm sorry I didn't understand that

you were trying to warn me that I could never be
Kanye because there is a cost to loving Black people
and especially Black women that he has decided
he doesn't need to pay. I'm scared, G. Everything I
tried to write away is still the house I'm standing in.
I made a home out of my pain, I'm sorry. I don't know
how I'mma get this thesis done, I don't know how
long I can survive like this. I don't think I want to
survive like this but I don't know what else there is.
I'm trying to let him go, I'm trying to leave that hurt
behind me but I'm also tryna reckon with it. I don't
know, nigga, I'm scared, I'm so scared and I'm a
whole chorus of sorry. I wish I knew what to ask you.
Nah, fuck that. I wish I had the courage to ask you
what I meant to last night: That we in Mississippi,
this state that we both got roots in, and that mean
we come from survivors who come from survivors
who come from an etc. I lost in the smoke. I know
we survivors, I know I'm a survivor and I know how
survival is a choice we made; but do you ever worry,
truly, that you chose wrong?

I remember looking up, the yawn of a branch heavy with
magnolias released petals too heavy to be feathers as I de-
leted everything and sent this instead:

I love you, thank you for not deciding to stop loving
me, you were right. Cudi verses on *Kids See Ghosts*
was way better. Ye never coming back.

The August air bristled with wasps the night Kanye
West came to Soldier Field to make one last burning ship for
his mother. The moonlight spilled over the trees and the heat
clung to the last of the summer while I was stuck in traffic,
just like the rest of the city. I knew by then who Kanye was,
but I was already in the process of writing a series of poems
all titled "The Book of Yeezus" to try and make sense of my
instinct to gild elegy, to give every death mask a set of grills.
So the show was—at some level—for "work." But if I'm being honest, it was also that I had seen Kanye live twice: once
for the Yeezus Tour in Brooklyn and a second time for Made
in America in Philly, but the Kanye show I'd always regretted missing came in 2007 during his Glow in the Dark Tour.
The concert was the same day my father and I packed some
clothes and hustled our car up to Minneapolis to see if I
could clinch a last second spot at the high school I'd eventually graduate from. I'd never seen Kanye in Chicago and it
didn't feel like a thing to die without seeing. It was the novel
I had never read, and I wouldn't know if it could be perfect
unless I came to see what he'd made of the grief that naming
the album "Donda" promised.

The rollout for *Donda* was some weird shit even by Kanye
standards, and we are now in the years where that is perhaps
the point. After a horrific episode running for president, saying all types of utter nonsense about slave nets, Kanye had
been mercifully silent for a stretch before rumblings began
that Kanye was working on an album named after his mother.
I didn't believe it for real until Kanye moved into the Mercedes-Benz dome in Atlanta putting on shows where clips

circulated of this nigga, my once-idol, running around in circles in a cape while poorly captured audio garbled around him. I had a feeling that whatever was going to happen when I saw Kanye at Soldier Field was going to shift my understanding of his work the way seeing the stagecraft of the Yeezus Tour made me finally like the murky, tortured amps of that album. And I wanted to understand, even after all this time, I just wanted to understand. So I paid way too much money for a ticket to go see Kanye grieve harmoniously.

But I wasn't going anywhere as the Lyft I was stuck in inched piecemeal through bumper-to-bumper traffic that ran up Lakeshore Drive, a sprawling pastoral of red lights each with an equally pissed-off driver inside that car. Even still, it was all good in the gentrified hood because all of Twitter said despite me being over an hour late, so was Kanye. Typical boy who thinks himself a god, working diligently to invent his own destruction—then vanishing.

I want to spare you my pulse. I want to spare you the description of the traffic congealed so badly that CPD demanded my driver let me out damn near two blocks from the stadium and the thud swelling in my ears as a stadium of cries dotted the air and I knew Kanye must have just come out because the screams hang in the air like birds. I want to spare you my pulse and the ache once more of my knees as I am once again running towards a grief I didn't author. And the seer of my body as I hustle up three flights of stairs because even the nosebleed section of this show costs fuckin bank, my torn hip burning until it is a kind of singing. One day it will be the melody of one bone against another, and that sound will one day maybe grow louder than whatever voice I have left. And I just know by the last flight of steps that one day my pain will be the loudest thing about me and what exactly does it cost for the mind to release what the body is forced to mourn? All of this matters, and none of it matters because finally I'm at the top of the steps, the closing notes of "Jail" dissolving in the air when I see that Kanye West has rebuilt his childhood home in the middle of Soldier Field.

Some grief defies metaphor, some grief starves without it. I was prepared for a nigga in a cape, I was prepared to witness something like the final shot of *Jeen-yuhs* where Kanye is lifted into the ceiling of the Mercedes-Benz dome, light in all directions holding the smoke captive, the boy rising into his grief while the ash beneath splayed wide as the arms of a magnolia. I wasn't prepared for the house. And from the distance I could see the shapes of men come and go from Kanye's mother's porch and I couldn't see that Kanye had enlisted another wealthy abuser in Marilyn Manson to sit a spell with him and DaBaby. While I sat between swaggering northside boys in old Yeezus tees, confederate flags cracked like mud across their chests, I stared and took notes. And in the rasp of Soldier Field's shitty speakers wheezing out elegy after bass-heavy elegy it was briefly all something like good—until Kanye West caught on fire.

Now, it's worth noting that this wasn't the original plan, but the original plan is not *less* absurd. Reportedly, Kanye's plan was to pay to dig out the roots of his actual childhood home and have it hauled across the entire city and installed in the middle of the field. The city of Chicago was . . . less enthused about this plan. And so Kanye built a model of the house and asked the city of Chicago for permission to light the house on fire. Lori Lightfoot and all thirty-four of her Steve Harvey suits were even less enthused about this plan given that Soldier Field is, well . . . a field, made of very flammable grass and limited exits. And so Kanye did what he always does, what I once did in slam and what I fear I am doing with you, even now, with this book of my preemptive and contemporary griefs, he turned mourning into spectacle. When there was no house to set fire to, he turned the flame on himself.

And there was something about watching Kanye on fire, though I had no idea that it even was really him because I figure most billionaires have a nigga they can pay to be on fire for them in the same way they have people they pay to be sorry on their behalf. And just like that, watching the flames die around his kerosene-soaked shoulder pads, I heard in my head:

There will never be enough hands to beat the earth.

I thought at first it must have been one of the MAGA-lite northsiders, but it was me—it was always me. Like Kanye, I have traded my pain for the kind of pain that folds. Like Kanye, I have refused the help and hands of people who love me in pursuit of some unbearable song. I have aspired to stop a city with my grief, because I was most visible when I was in pain. But watching the pixelated flames that danced over the recreated house as the stadium drained, white boys dripped with secession and Jordans so ugly they can only be custom made disappearing like the ghosts they wore into the arena. There will never be enough hands to beat the earth and never enough earth to make it worthwhile. I don't always know how to leave this instinct, but I can and I will because I must.

I cannot live my life or make my art as the kind of boi who drags his life behind him. I have lived that life, it is the most famous image of me and maybe always will be, I touched the hem of that kind of notoriety and it nearly cost me my entire life to be in that kind of pain for a living that wasn't even a living. The flames sputtered as the projector cut to black and Kanye disappeared into the mouth of the stadium, but the image clung to my eyes for hours after—that this may be what it costs to grow, to embrace living not merely as an appendage of my grief, to hear Kanye almost humming, *O love, o love, for you, I burn the house.*

ELENA

Dear Elena,

It was mid-February in Mississippi when I watched you in your stark-white tuxedo swaying to a song. Then your mami, brother, landlord and abuela all joined in the waltz, and in the midst of that love, I saw you bright as a swan—by Mississippi standards, the only snow for miles. And it just made me want to cry, y'know? All that beauty, all that us, all this distance between me and my own mother.

In many ways, when you came across the screen of *One Day at a Time* you were the representation I'd been looking for for years, the queer Latinx teen that I never could bring myself to be. By the time I saw you, it felt like it was already too late. Not because it was season two, because I felt I was too late to be me. I felt that dance was already impossible.

Elena, my mother doesn't dance. Not "doesn't like" to dance; *doesn't* dance, so don't ask her.

Story goes that when my mother was a little
girl she was dancing with her sisters at a party in
Washington Heights. Nobody can agree on what the
party was for, just that it was some occasion that
brought all the daughters of the families that fled
Trujillo together. For that moment, my mother and
her sisters were just girls and a song. Story goes that
my mother was never a gifted dancer, that Abuelo
laughed from the corner. Story goes that after that
laugh, my mother never danced again aside from
once or twice at her wedding.

In the only photo of the wedding I've seen, on New
Year's Eve 1984, she is standing and smiling next
to my father. He is taller and wearing a smile that
the flash washes out of his eyes. She is wearing an
amber dress, the color of dusk. Outside, past the little
courthouse, I imagine dusk in Washington Heights.
When I arrived in this world, the sun had already
set on my chance to sway with my mother like you
did on-screen with yours, like daughters of the same
distance, quietly bridging the gap between what
happened and what ought to be.

———————

Dear Elena,

Once, I had an abuelo. I never came out to him,
mostly because we didn't speak the same language.

He came to America in the 1950s *porque* he told a
joke. I should clarify, he told a joke about Rafael
Leónidas Trujillo, the Dominican Republic's
president for life. And it was just a joke, and it was
just his friends but it wasn't. Nobody knows how the
joke got back to Trujillo's secret police but soon they
began to pull around, black VW beetles glistening
like the bodies of castanets, to ask where he was.
And so the story was that my abuela had to finesse
her green card and fly alone across the ocean,
pulling their home along behind her until eventually
they were in New York and my abuelo could become
my mother's father.

For a long time, my fluency was running up
against the clock of my abuelita's death. She spoke
almost exclusively Spanish, and never said my
name without a grin. She had vertigo, and even
when her world spun right, all my words came at
the wrong angles, no matter how much I rehearsed.
When I learned that she died, I was in the back of
a car hurtling through a field in Iowa, a long yawn
of wheat—golden as any heaven. But all I felt was
my Spanish withering in my mouth as I realized
I'd missed my chance to say "I love you" without
rehearsal, my name with perfect clarity.

Elena, I guess I'm wondering if you ever felt the
same worry: that when you opened your mouth all
that you were would fall out in the wrong language.
That perhaps there is no fluency to be found, the

right words may never exist. I'm wondering if as the
only out-queers in our immediate families, you know
that we share the concern in our mothers' eyes; the
sweat that gilds their palms. We share their silence.
That expansive quiet that means they love us, but are
afraid of how it will translate.

———————

Dear Elena,

It's worth noting that I've never heard my mother
sing. Not one note, not in three decades. Growing
up she was quiet and even when she dragged me
to church with her, the choir swallowed the psalms
she lent her voice to. My mother spent much of my
childhood swearing she was tone-deaf, that there
wasn't a single musical bone in her body but for
whatever reason I didn't want to believe her. To
me there was a song inside everything she did.
The rhythm of her Spanish, the brisk melody with
which she called my name. Where she was, the air
hummed. There was a song inside my mother, I was
certain—at her core, a note that lasted forever.

   There's a bottle episode in the middle of season
one of *One Day at a Time* where the only character
that never leaves the room is the constantly ringing
house phone. It thrums again and again as your
mother tries to get her VA rep on the phone so that

she can see a doctor that will make living hurt less
on a daily basis. I remember this even though I was
not present for it. I remember because I don't have
any memories of my mother not in pain. I remember
wondering if you did.

Since I was a child I resemble my mother, and
according to her I have my abuelo's hands. I used
those hands to massage her pain as he once did. I'd
never seen a Latina in pain on TV like our mothers,
even though most Latina moms sing better and
clearer than J. Lo. The closest I ever got to hearing
Momma sing for years was the long sighs that came
with me trying to use my small hands to unbind the
muscles in her back. I played her tendons like a
harp, diligently hunting for the sound that meant I
was helping.

What did you make of the grunts and winces
of your mami, Elena? These shudders that made a
music of her; the phone call on hold for as long as
you can remember. The dial tone hanging in the
air—the lowest form of bird, the lowest form of song.

But there was a night in 2009 where I thought
I'd finally caught a note through the door. I was
your age, I wore college hoodies I would never
need and grimaced from knee pain everywhere
that I stepped. And through the door of my parents'
bedroom, I could hear a noise, one long sustained
noise that crested and fell like waiting room music.
And because I'm dramatic, because I wanted to

know everything there was to know about my mother
I stopped at the door and pressed my ear to the
bubbled white paint. I wanted more than anything
to know the words to the song that made my mother
sound even more like my mother.

But there were no lyrics because there was no
song.

There's a nerve in the back called the sciatica,
and in my mother that night it throbbed. I came
through the door to ask my mother what she was
singing and found her curled at the bottom edge of
her bed. A moan of pain rose and fell out of her,
always straight shouldered and now curled until she
was no bigger than a comma. I knelt at my mother's
side, pulse scattering in all directions. This is the
night my mother teaches me that some pains never
leave you, that you can never unhear the sound of
your mother coming apart at the nerves. It was a
while before she could wrench her eyes open to look,
really look, me in the eyes with her mouth still full
of silent prayers I mistook for lyrics. Words in a song
that goes "mercy, mercy, mercy" and its lone note
goes on forever.

What makes the episode "Hold, Please" stick in
my heart, ultimately, is that dial tone. It is strange
the music we wring from waiting. As I sat with my
father in the emergency room waiting area with
my mother trying desperately to muffle her pain.
Until eventually she couldn't take the pain of sitting

normally a second longer and bent over a table at a
90 degree angle. Because it was all that could quiet
the sciatica's song even a little. Only then, because
the nursing staff said they'd never seen a person have
to manage pain like that, did they finally take her
inside. Meanwhile, the dial tone of the desk hummed
its same three notes as they eased her through the
door. It fucks with you too, right? The tune of your
mother's agony coming in ten-second increments.
Was it present as you accidentally came out, on-
screen for the first time? Elena, in the absence of
our mothers, could we have expected more song than
this? The dial tone, the waiting, the indignity of an
invisible pain with a root whose name, like sciatica,
you have to sing a little to pronounce. In the space
between rings, I wish I'd known your mother sounds
just like mine; that you sounded just like me—right
down to conversations it seemed we'd only ever have
with the air.

————

Dear Elena,

I first imagined telling my parents that I was bisexual
on a bus to Providence on June 13, 2016. If you
know what that means without my saying it, then
we probably live in the same history—cousins by
virtue of the same grief. The bus swayed past acres

of green. The morning after the Pulse shooting was aesthetically a day like any other. To my parents it was a tragic day, but not the kind of tragic that made them think immediately about where their son might be.

I scrolled through the growing list of the murdered. Scrolled through reports saying the shooter was a regular at the bar he massacred. And in a year where all my dreams were of death, and all my waking thoughts too, I had always imagined in these dreams that whoever mourned me, mourned who the world knew me to be. And as the engine roiled beneath my seat, the June air seeping with heat, I knew that I couldn't live my life in the closet. If I was going to live I needed it to be as myself, if I was going to die I wanted to be mourned as a whole. I knew that when I returned home I would have to give my parents something else to worry about.

I wanted my coming out to feel the way I imagine it would've felt if my mother had been the one who taught me to dance, if she had been the one who took my small hands in hers and did what she has always done. If my hand was in hers, my mother grinning at my forward steps and being gentle with my retreats. In reality, it was mostly quiet. I told my parents that I was bisexual and my mother reacted like yours, she grinned, she nodded and my father said that was all well and good but I had still promised to help him move a shelf so it'd be cool if we wrapped this up.

Just like that, before the commercial break of the
sitcom they were watching ended, I had stepped into
the rest of my life.

———————

Dear Elena,

Y'all really did have an episode for everything,
and when Mississippi's muted green winter thawed
into the beginnings of another relentless summer I
convinced my mother to watch *One Day at a Time*
with me. Just the two of us, my head on her shoulder,
watching the daughter I never was.
    In this episode, she is watching me dance with
my first same-sex partner at prom. In this life, we
are arguing about me mentioning that I am queer
in my artist bio. In this episode, she is holding my
hand while I tell her how lonely it is when the world
is more equipped to love you than your own family.
In this life, my mother is reminding me that all
she knows about where I live are the bodies that
floated from the river. She asks me what I'm doing
in Mississippi, I tell her I'm looking for a whole town
bent around a question. In this life, she is telling
me to be quiet because she is afraid that my need
to live fully as myself may have killed her only son.
In a season finale, we are both standing at Abuela's
hospital bed, as we did in our real life at my abuelo's,

praying in different languages for the chance to say goodbye. It's not a perfect comparison, nothing on-screen could ever hope to hold everything my mother is. But it's been a chance, for a half hour at a time, for me to let her into this other place where we are swaying slowly to a song I know but can't translate, this dance I do alone to remember who she is.

———

Dear Elena,

I misspoke in my last letter, there was an episode for everything except me, except Afro-Latinx people. Throughout the run of *One Day at a Time*, the Alvarezes covered everything from immigration to chronic pain to a remarkably ill-advised and poorly constructed 9-11 episode, but no Black Latinos ever come up in the show. We never even smile next to y'all, never say our names and see them held by the same melody and respect as yours.

Honestly, I have grown bored of being the specter of Latinx media. Of being unseen even as I'm seen. I do not need to ask why the show chose not to see us, I was born already knowing. I need to know when you will choose to see us, I'm weary of the quiet that comes with asking to be seen.

It feels almost fitting that the last time I saw you, I didn't. Not the normal way but rather dressed as

an animated self. I suppose the pandemic warped us
all in different ways. I suppose that we can only ask
so much of what it is to feel seen, to feel loved even
by an imperfect mirror. I watched the final episode
of *One Day at a Time*, an experiment in animation
that put the once and future President Pendejo right
in its sights. And with that final breath, after three
cancellations, the show was finally over. It was
quiet as the snow that dusted Mississippi that first
February I watched you sway with your mother the
way I once ached to sway with mine. My mother who
loved this show and seeing you, and loved the bridge
it built between who I once was and who I love now.

At the end of you, the moral was always my
mother. The moral was always her hand, which I find
in mine again, and once more.

RETURN of the
ELECTRIC SAD BOY

i. All the Kids at the Bat Mitzvah
Love the Bartender

If you, like me, were thirteen in the Year of Our Auto-tune 2007, you were sure of two things and only two things: (1) *I am always sorry and I never know for what* and (2) *Damn, T-Pain is truly a legend.* If you, like me, are someone who has never been especially confident about the fact that you have a body, then maybe you sat at the edge of a ring of children your own age at a bat mitzvah. Maybe you were the only one who was expected to dance. Maybe, when the DJ called "snowball," you danced with the girl at the center of the whole party. And the girl was taller than you and maybe a few years or ancestors ago it would have been illegal for you to touch her.

But you were invited.

In full view of her parents at the country club, against the dark polished oak of the walls, where already you were learning that adolescence is really just knowing where you are not supposed to be, you placed your hands on the sides of her taller hips as T-Pain crooned, "I like the bartender." The girl smiled and it sounded, amid all those eyes, like someone had dropped a knife directly on its point and sampled only the best of melody. She guided my hands, which were still not touching her but just kinda orbiting near where she wasn't. Her eyes almost pitying, as if to say, *It's OK, I promise nothing sharps exists here.* And I believed it, because it was the year of the body. The year where my voice became my voice, where I lost the high notes, the only reason two women would ever fight over me. But my hands stayed fists through the whole dance, and maybe this is something you can remember if you've ever been beckoned to a song you couldn't make good on. How the nails burrow small horizons into the palm, bleach the pink briefly from the flesh until something is setting in your hand; maybe this is where we both enter, at this tenderness I was sure must draw blood.

For nearly half a decade, T-Pain was a mainstay on every radio, at every school dance, on every iPod, or, in my case, iPod knockoff. Everyone knew when he was coming from the unmistakable twinge of auto-tune. Faheem Rashad Najm was born and remains a very talented singer. But back in the early 2000s, T-Pain was so good at riding the warbly undercurrents of his auto-tuned voice that I thought it was an entirely separate person doing the introduction to *Nappy Boy*

Radio. In my eyes there are two T-Pains, and I've grown to love both, but at thirteen, and even now if I'm being honest with you, I preferred this tinny caricature that made it feel like anybody could sing.

Ironically, auto-tune was not developed with an ear towards the human voice. Andy Hildebrand, its creator, made the technology with the intent to use it for oil drilling. "Autocorrelation" was meant to map the earth at a potential drilling site and, using the reverberations beneath the ground, accurately identify the best spot to drill. But eventually Hildebrand realized how auto-tune could serve the music industry, and he departed those scorching oil fields for plush recording studios. Auto-tune's aim was originally quite simple; it was not supposed to be an effect, but rather a mistake eraser. And who hasn't longed for a bridge between what their voice could do and what they intended it to do?

T-Pain dropped "I'm Sprung" in the prolific stick of August 2005 and then "I'm N Luv (Wit a Stripper)." A hundred tweens mimicking T-Pain snapped our fingers and danced in place elaborately to a song about a place we were under no circumstances legally allowed to set foot in. I like the idea that T-Pain knew the history of auto-tune; I like a narrative in which he gilded his voice with a melody first designed to find where the dead had whittled themselves down to fuel.

Oil is a story about what becomes more valuable in obscurity. This is also the story for me and the other three Black boys on the eighth-grade DC trip. Our role, since we weren't rich or white, was to be the center for the culture. I was particularly close to two other Black boys in the grade.

I treasured that little archipelago we formed in the back of half our classes, this space where we were us and that was enough. We were expected to know each new hot song, our dance moves crisp to the point of rehearsal but organic to the point of instinct. We joked about sitting in the back of the bus. We knew we were put here to cull a choice from unlivable weather, that this was old Black work. We reveled in the new-old cool of our bodies, as if we chose to be us.

Drafts of intimacy don't always hold up though and we learned how to "other" long before we learned how to be gentle. This time it was over the fact that I am also Dominican and, at the time, this seemed divorceable from Blackness. I was divorceable. It all came to a head on the eighth-grade DC trip when they remembered that I was not "all Black," like they were. I wasn't allowed to sit in the back of the bus anymore. We'd been squad, a common music, and now there was only the silence after one of the boys I called my brother called me a half-breed.

In a misguided attempt to impress a girl, I started scaling the taller arm of a big-ass statue. I touched a scalding spot and ya boi fell hard and the screen of my bootleg Zune was shattered. When I desperately shoved the aux cord into the port something was playing, still.

In another essay, this might be about resilience. But this ain't that essay.

The screen of the shitty little knock-off was unsalvageable, pixelated in parts but mostly white, not like snow but the edge of a scar. Song or no song, it was clear that there could be no return from what had happened.

It goes like this most of the flight, my eyes closed trying to remember what letter of the alphabet I'm on. All I am craving, with my small draft of true abandonment, is a voice that moans *Shawty* tender and somehow with static at the edges. Eventually, amber streetlights gild the bottom of clouds, an army of chrysanthemums passing below me as the plane descends. I never tell anyone that one of my once-friends hit me in the mouth with his belt, trying to school me in "real Black people discipline." In exchange I never told him how "belt" is another verb for song. It stays this way until a year later I punch him. Because we were Black American boys who aspired to be American men, this was what makes us friends again. It is not the last time I've been made vulnerable by loyalty. Maybe though it is the first time I crave an emotional distance from my own voice. That I want to let less people in. I carry my name like a bruise in my mouth. Maybe you know this too, reader, what it is when something wounds you and the blood doesn't spill for a whole year.

ii. Reporting Live from Distance, October 20-something

In the Year of Our Auto-tune 2010 Drake was proof that, to a degree, you never needed to stop being sixteen; you just needed to sing better. You can hear the influence of auto-tune and especially Kanye West's *808's & Heartbreak* on tracks like "Lust for Life" or "Houstatlantavegas," the blueprint for Drake songs that are all promises and gut-heavy drums. The beats that come to us from an entrenched sadness, what many men drape in shadow and simply hope goes away. I have been that man and now I'm no man at all. It is the sound that comes after the liquor we can't pronounce briefly drowns the name we can, but would rather not.

I don't remember when I first heard Drake but I remember who I was, a very sad Black boy dreaming of spring. A thing about Minnesota is that you hear about the winter before you hear about anything else. And if you have never lived through a Minnesota winter maybe you don't realize that a season is as much an act of faith as it is anything else. In Minnesota, it'll dead be negative 20 for two straight days. My senior year of high school I woke up one morning with my mother sitting at the end of my bed, and last time that happened somebody died. That time? It was because it snowed so hard the night before that the roof of the Metrodome collapsed, and school was canceled for the fourth time in my entire life. Sometimes I think snow like that is the closest God comes to speaking in complete sentences.

I was sixteen when "So Far Gone" dropped when Drake's fame was still so fragile. Anywhere that gave me permission to lose a layer was a tenderness. I was good at acting like I was thrilled to be wherever I was but the whole thing was a front. I was auto-tuning to what I thought people wanted from me, I sang from the wrong places. I kept singing from those wrong places even when it hurt, sometimes I wanted it to hurt. We were so fragile. We are so fragile. I walked the streets of my Minneapolis suburb, headphones locked in on "Successful," dreaming of spring.

Drake is many things, one of those things is the patron saint of the Male Pick-Me Anthem. The formula for most Drake songs about women is roughly the same: Drake is the hazy protagonist, the prototypical sad boi. He just wants *better* for whoever is the girl listening to the song, live from somewhere. He does this in the club, in the car, in an old letterman jacket. I did it on the bus, on the train, in the back of the classroom.

Drake was an alternate boyhood, one where it was sadness that made us pretty. Our resentment that assured us that we were in the right. This is also a kind of faith, a bad season. The early Drake beats felt too soft to be about blame, though they are. Ultimately, Drake wants you to know that we are sorry, even though we never apologized. And if you don't accept that, we will make you sorry by becoming more famous than you and writing your name into songs we would never sing to your face.

I fucked up, I sang into this for years.

Drake is not known most for his auto-tune, but like the technology he helped a younger me become deft at finding the soft point in a sentence and make the narrative mine. The boy I was and the man I can still be at times believes that very little is actually my fault. The hard thing of growing up is learning, again and again, how rare it is that anything is only one person's fault. Reader, at times it is me who has dropped the knife, me who has sampled and looped only the best of how I am complicit in what has hurt us both.

In my first real heartbreak, I was quick to share that once I was cheated on by someone I was planning to marry.

I wanted to own it, that hurt, make it sing high and only for me. I was slower to offer that somewhere along the line, me and my ex had made each other responsible for our living. I can be slow to acknowledge that part, where we were both unfair. I was too willing to follow something that I could see was hurting us both. It was their decision to burn down what we were building, it was my decision to stay in the house long after the first match was dropped. I'm still trying to learn how to let go and I fail more often than I don't.

Drake is easiest to believe if you have faith that you are always the protagonist of your own sadness. And once, I thought I was owed this too. I believed that every winter has a protagonist. I didn't know for sure if grief ought to have a protagonist, but where I didn't know, I imagined the wrong thing and became it so many times. I thought I was the hero, though at times I was, and can still be, the winter.

iii. Turns Out My Favorite T-Pain Song Is "A Change Is Gonna Come"

He's escorted in, as always, by something familiar but still not what it once was. The opening notes of the iconic Sam Cooke song "A Change Is Gonna Come" are higher, opening the door for sweeping strings. It's not what we're used to with T-Pain on the mic, it almost sounds like the keys themselves are anxious. And I imagine, maybe, T-Pain was nervous then too. It'd been a decade since his first album, a year since he sat and sang various hits on the most popular episode of

NPR's *Tiny Desk* ever, a capella. My nigga, accompanied only by expectation. I don't know if he was nervous, but I know he must have been nervous. T-Pain has shared in the past that he's never worked with a vocal coach, that he knows he has sung from the wrong place for years to the point he loses his voice multiple times a year. But to change that risks losing what made him a legend, he learned to love that hurt but what if tonight is the night it buckles all together. It's what happens when you trust your own voice—it can fail you, it can fail you in front of everybody.

But this is triumph music, earned melody. T-Pain, clad in a button-down shirt and a tie with a buckle winking like a shared joke beneath his chin, is good from the very first note. And watching from my own small room, now deep in my twenties, I begin to cry. Like I said, I am always sorry for something and most of getting older has been figuring out why. On this day, I'm crying because I doubted him, and still he made room for me inside one of my favorite songs.

Tenderness has been as much about making space for failure as anything. Beyond the room in which I write this, it's one of the hottest summers ever written. Most of what I've grieved all my life is still alive, and where it isn't I'm trying to be gentle with what notes they left behind. On-screen T-Pain singing of a change until he sang in another country altogether.

I hope wherever you are you find a moment like this someday. I promise—everything is tender, nothing is bleeding.

OF TENDERNESS,
OF FUGITIVES

I have a talent for making fugitives out of anything is a line I found buried in the notes of a class I took my first year in Oxford, Mississippi. I thought about fugitives often that first year, wading through the darkness between Oxford's streetlights. The bird rattling the branches above my midnight walk home? Fugitive. The river's endless march towards elsewhere? Fugitive. The yawn of the oak above me asking what I'm doing in Mississippi? You see where I'm going with this, you see the question I'm related to. I get questions about fugitives a lot when I explain my "re-migration," the confused stares and jokes of how much ancestral work I've unspooled just by being in Mississippi. Condescension towards Mississippi became a low buzz that year. Night in Mississippi is like nowhere else, since that first year in my dreams all the woods are thrumming with fugitives.

Oxford, in the hands of another writer, is a particular kind of gorgeous. It is a long and vibrant sentence about the courthouse at the town center, the low roar of the stadium which drifts over everything on a Saturday, crowding the sky until it bullies the sun out of hiding and spills gold over Faulkner's Rowan Oak, and the long string of men who follow his call.

This story ain't about none of that shit.

Instead I want to tell you a story that starts with me almost missing my bus. And Devin Hester.

Across the years, I've learned how to be bored in a seminar class. I was taking a graduate seminar about being a grad student and when things got too meta I just went on YouTube. The key to watching a video when you're bored in class, besides not having reflective glasses on, is to never watch anything that you're seeing for the first time. I have two videos that are my go-to when I want to check out, but not clearly be out of rhythm with the class. The first is Devin Hester's 2007 Super Bowl opening kick-off touchdown return. When I watch it I'm not hearing the iconic "DEVIN HESTER YOU ARE RIDICULOUS!!" or even the roar of the Bears fans as we took our first and only lead of Super Bowl XLI. I'm hearing the memory of hearing my dad holler, *"Nigga"* at the top of his lungs for the very first time.

In eighth grade my dad and I lived in an apartment alone on the north side of Chicago while my mom was trapped back in Omaha, Nebraska, hoping a house we'd been pressured into buying would sell. It was 2007, it did not sell. So that meant many weekends with me curled in the back seat of the car I'd eventually drive to Water Valley, Mississippi.

My father drove us back and forth to Omaha so I wouldn't be totally without my mom.

Dad generally cut down his "Nigga" usage rate so I wouldn't have to fight the kind of white boys who would take me saying "Nigga" as a kind of permission. He of course had the quick "Nigga" under his breath from time to time, more of a grunt than a word. There was the disbelieving fastball, "Nigga, you done split your tongue into five different lies" on the phone with his childhood friends. But generally, him saying "Nigga" was a rarity if he knew I was listening. But on the night of the Super Bowl, it was just the two of us and some miracles you can only admire with a small curse.

Devin Hester simply had *It* the night in Miami when he stood stretching at the edge of the end zone, hoping against hope that something everyone who worked for the Colts had sworn wouldn't happen would happen anyway. Hester had a reputation for miracles, for his one-man demolition job on the Arizona Cardinals which produced the infamous Dennis Green rant, one of the all-time funniest press conferences in sports history. Hester was like a dancer, and everywhere he stepped grown men fell to their knees and wept at the prodigious boy, fugitive from half the men on the field gliding into the end zone as if nothing might ever touch him again. The kick rises and Hester's legs are churning even as the stitch of the ball spins, a single magnolia petal, floating into his outstretched arms.

Hester has a magic trick he does that I don't know many people notice as anything but a miracle. He chops his legs hard in the early going of a run, creating a hummingbird-like illusion that he's already built to full speed, but it's all a mirage. The minute his pursuers slow to launch for him is when he's really running & now my father is pounding the arms of his chair as Hester explodes out & into the open field and the fugitive in both of us sees yardage and thinks *Free* thinks *Go* thinks *Home* shouts over and over, "Run nigga run, run like you stole something" until the thud of his fists is a percussion, the splintering wood, his high hat & Hester is our kin because that is all that nigga means in our mouth & our mouths are the only ones that matter & they're over-stuffed with sound because an impossible thing is happening & Hester has a whole choir, a whole chain of running, an endless train of teammates, and a retired Deion Sanders sprinting along the sideline & they're a song that swells across the whole country & it takes 13.5 seconds in total, yet the harmony of it stretches for the rest of my life.

Dark smudges over the Oxford sky as ten years later the video ends and I realize someone in class has launched into a lengthy and fairly racist monologue about slave narratives. The form of the slave narrative begins often with "I was born" and eventually the escape from what one was born to. I suppose we are all attempting to outrun something. In this case I was just trying to outrun the clock because the thing about Mississippi is that I needed a car, but I needed groceries and rent more.

Class ended on someone discussing their research on Iggy Azalea being used as the premise for an academic paper on what Black people sound like. Meanwhile, I needed to be out exactly on time, otherwise I would miss the last

bus off campus. And on this particular night, with the
heat of the morning turning to ghosts, I stepped outside to
see the last bus of the night whipping around the corner.
Which, if I missed it, meant a two-mile uphill walk through
the dark in a Mississippi I'd only been in for a month. I did
what I always do, I ran—I ran with the desperation of a
nigga who isn't worried about how ridiculous you look running with a backpack stuffed with a laptop & two classes
of grading even though I technically only teach one class,
but I'm trying to cover for someone because we're all we
got & the bus is too far & my knees have ached for the last
three generations & that pain means the only thing I hate
more than motion is standing still & I'm thinking of Devin
Hester and feeling the hummingbird thrum of my busted
tendons screeching against each other when five, yes five,
Black boys I don't know from Adam see me running & we
live out an old joke, that nothing makes Black people run
faster than seeing other Black people running & how they
saw me in that near pitch darkness is a question I leave
to the ancestors, who are all running with us now, as the
boys sprint next to me their ball shorts swirling at their
knees like the flags of nations we may never deserve & they
must have been balling for hours before we became kin
in this moment where they saw me and turned so the boy
who was in the back of their procession is now the front,
sprinting neck and neck with the engine and hollering of
a boy, a boy, a boy at the back who needs to come on &
the bus driver who has left me three times already that
semester nods & he passes the message down the length of

our running, our uninterrupted chain and each of them is pumping their arms, chanting to me some version of "Run, nigga run, they'll wait, they'll wait, we got you, run, nigga" and so I do—I sprint through that tenderness into their harmony, & found myself cousin to boys I will never see again.

One of the most frustrating things about doing this project in the long twilight of my grandmother's life was that by the time I was born, she was already in no real state to answer the questions I didn't yet know to ask. The interior life of a fugitive is often hard to access, and there are costs to the attempt to portray it. There's a way the life of a fugitive can be flattened only to their escape, only to the bloodied percussion of feet that hammer the ground with their desperation to be if not free, then at least free of where they were.

For this reason, I'll never know what was said to my grandmother, age four, the day her father must have come home from work, maybe a touch sweatier than usual. I can only imagine that he and his wife sat in a room, stuffing suitcases with hushed voices, holding each other's hands with a particular tenderness I've mostly seen exchanged by Black people who have just learned that wherever they have stayed is now a place they have stayed too long.

This occurs to me in November of 2019 as me and the homies pile into the car to see *Queen & Slim*, a film that is, theoretically, about Black fugitives falling in love after accidentally killing a cop who was un-accidentally trying to kill them. Writer Lena Waithe described the couple's flight from Ohio to Florida as a kind of inverted Underground Railroad, and I was intrigued by that if nothing else. None of us know that this will be a film about Black pain that mostly succeeds in creating more Black pain.

Beauty alone was not enough. *Queen & Slim* has many faults but maybe nothing as bad as the ending. And it's one all of us see coming, but maybe at different points. For me, it wasn't the scene where Queen and Slim have a prolonged sex scene, in front of a graveyard while a protest tears apart the small town they just fled. It wasn't the child who dies blowing a police officer away, the same boy who tells the two gorgeous fugitives that it's OK if they don't make it because then they're legends and icons. And it should've been that, if I'm keeping it a buck. Because the movie just moves on from this child so in love with martyrdom that he became one. All I'm saying is that if there was time to ride horses, there was certainly time to try and answer the Black question of what it means to be infinite against your will. To be an icon when you only wanted a handful of normal years; a hand to hold in the midst of running, even with the destination wreathed in the dark beyond your headlights' reach.

It was a quiet scene where Slim was telling Queen about his hopes and aspirations. That's when I knew, one way or another, this brother was marked for death. Because it's a common trope. I took an informal poll of all my friends on what they feel when the character who looks like them starts talking about their hopes and dreams. Almost to a fault, the answer was the same: this character is about to die, and they are going to die brutally. I feel this pull sometimes. Sometimes when I am talking about my ambitions I'm really just touching on an old trope about movies and TV that if you see the rehearsal of a performance, you will never see the performance. At the end, all things cut to black.

Huddled into my cramped Minneapolis studio after the movie, each of us are trying to find the words for how *Queen & Slim* cracked something inside us—the movie ends approximately three times before it actually ends. And none of them are the right ending. At the end of two hours of frantic running, slow dancing, and slipping out of attic windows, the duo are ultimately betrayed on the runway to their plane by a Black grilled-out Florida man who closes the film counting the stacks of money he's raked in, grinning a snitch's smile.

We watch the bullets fly, we watch the white girl pull the trigger, all things fade to black and this might have been the end of the movie. In some lives I wouldn't have had to hold a woman I love like my own sister as she asked tearfully what is the function of Black creators if so many will treat us exactly like white creators do. In another life, the hands that wrote this lynching don't look a shade or two away from mine. But then there's a lengthy funeral sequence, and another fade to black. Then a reveal of a massive mural of the murdered protagonists that all ultimately smacks of the same thing: the central question of the movie was irresolvable. We are irresolvable.

In a later interview Lena Waithe noted that in an earlier draft of the script it was a white woman who ultimately turns over Queen and Slim to the authorities, who then go on to do what authorities do. But she got some advice to follow what was most painful and the character turned into a man dripping in gold. Pain as a North Star to Queen and Slim even as they barreled farther south the whole movie, close as a razor to the path my own great-grandfather took to move his family to East St. Louis, migrations in two directions to get loose from the same problem. None of these are the right ending because the story really ends twenty minutes before Queen is murdered.

It's the moment that Kaluuya sticks his head out of the window of their car with all the light happy to hold him as he lets his eyes close. I don't think you can call it freedom, but for a moment, he doesn't know he's on the way to his death. He is a fugitive beneath the sun, but he and Queen are also alive and moving still. I wonder what it would have been like if *Queen & Slim* had been more of a story of tenderness, and only tenderness. A film where two Black people are brought together by the survival of violence but it doesn't become all that they are. I wanted to watch two Black people fall in love, not two Black characters murdered into becoming Black icons. And in that shot there was a chance to leave them, just like that, a crisp moon blooming across Kaluuya's face; the Black boy in love, briefly, with a world he will never see again.

There's a joke where God walks into a bar and it becomes my favorite love story about time. The way the alliance between my anxiety and my memory is set up, I really struggle with what it means to be present. Often, I am in another time even as I am speaking to you, even now. Everything I've loved and everything I've survived is already there simultaneous and loud. To me there is no progression. The idea of "past" is something I understand but not a thing I feel. Watching the penultimate episode of HBO's *Watchmen*, "A God Walks into Abar," I joke that I'm kind of a bootleg Doctor Manhattan in this way, if you retconned his ability to teleport, create life from nothing and live on Mars and replaced that with, well, mostly debilitating anxiety. Like Doctor Manhattan, I don't experience the concept of "before" in the way most people describe it to me, there is only layer upon layer of now.

The pandemic though, threw all that shit out of whack. I woke one morning and I couldn't look to the past for something similar I had survived. I couldn't see a future that I could describe as anything but "shrinking." I had a meticulous understanding of what it meant to be in control, and just like that, it was dust. I can still feel that despair because the pandemic is not over. Slowly all times were becoming hard times to live in. And after binging through every comfort show I had during quarantine, I finally started in on *Watchmen*.

"A God Walks into Abar" begins as your typical contemporary god meets Vietnam beat cop love story. Regina King's Angela Abar is skeptical that she's meeting the real Doctor Manhattan and so he tells her of a moon, and the Eden he made on it. Narration glides over violins, notes swelling with genesis, a whole world's creation pulling itself, blue fist over blue fist, into being before our eyes.

Adam and Eve in Doctor Manhattan's eyes are made in the image of the lord and lady of an enormous mansion where a young Doctor Manhattan once was sheltered as he and his father fled the Holocaust. And I understand a bit of what it feels like for a traumatic memory like this to always be happening to you, as real as what is in front of you. Doctor Manhattan is always at the moment he first laid eyes on Angela Abar, the woman he loves before they ever touch. I know what it means to Doctor Manhattan when the person he loves holds his face mid-argument and says, "John, when are you?" What has harmed me never feels far from me, every knife that has cut me still lives behind my eyes.

It is May 2022 and lately, the world is still terrible. But it's my partner's birthday week and they've never been to Mississippi before so we rent a car and I watch the magnolias like pearls in the kudzu as we whip towards Biloxi. I'm pointing to the shoreline and smelling this state where I've been a fugitive from much, including myself. But this feels different, a trip we're taking for the sake of how much I've fallen in love with the lavender scent of my partner's hair, her eyes the color of an autumn moon. There is a part of me now that is always here at this moment where I relearned Mississippi is a wonderful place to be in love. What it was to hold her for the first time, feel her voice against me as she asks, "When are you?" because my eyes are far away staring into the fog clinging to yellowed streetlights beyond our tiny balcony. But this time it is all visions of the future, our future. How lucky, to be at their side and see their many transformations, all the years we might have where the first thing I hear is how they say my name the way a morning glory opens its petals. My partner worries differently about the future than I do, it's one of the many ways their brain makes me feel more possible. They don't believe in knowing exactly what will happen, they believe in trying anyway. Even when my mind is everywhere that could tear us apart, she finds a little Eden in the unknown. I'm many years into the future when they tug my sleeve and ask again, "When are you?" The rain makes halos for every streetlight for miles, and I pull myself back to the time I'm present in. Because I choose them. I know that part of me will always be with this moment where the question matters so much more than the answer. Because the answer is almost always, everywhere.

Doctor Manhattan was doomed from the moment they met. He knows he will die, and he knows that the moment he fell in love with Angela is the moment that he told her that she could not save him from the men who have finally come to succeed at dismantling a god. That he loves her not because Regina King going straight Tom Clancy novel on at least eleven white supremacists is awe inspiring and heart-breaking in equal measure. He loves her for the attempt, that at the end of everything, she's going to try anyway. I'm writing this to you at a time of bad weather and worse news. Every day the world ends a little more and like any American I want to shelter in the past. Like any bootleg god, I want to build new worlds in my head and name them the future just to know what will happen.

But, I don't want that anymore. I want to hold my partner to my chest for as many days as I have a chest. I have no idea what will happen, I simply know that, like all relationships, they are there in the beginning of a stretch of time, and they are there at the end of it. I don't know what that end will be but my love, in the end, each time you have kissed me it has been the end of running; I am yours to make a shelter of, for you I forsake, however briefly, all other worlds.

Speaking of "the end," I realize now that I never told you the other video I love to watch when I'm supposed to be paying attention to something else. It's the "Never Catch Me" video by Flying Lotus. In the video two small Black children lie in matching caskets, the congregation's heads bowed in reverence for a small pair of lives clearly taken, though we'll never know how. As a Kendrick Lamar verse I sometimes find myself rapping without even noticing grinds into motion, both the boy and the girl sit bolt upright. They dance in perfect harmony, dipping and swirling like old leaves in new weather, like the light that shimmies away from the blade.

All the church is oblivious with grief and haven't I sometimes been too? Haven't I sometimes been so preoccupied with running, with a destination I can only call "elsewhere" and hope it is a kind of heaven? Haven't I too been guilty of missing the small ancestors pirouetting alongside me, clapping me towards Mississippi where summer begs the dead to dance and they oblige. When a Black boy dies, I think, *He could have been me, I could have been him.* And from this video, I wrote three of the poems in the MFA packet that brought me to Mississippi, and ain't that a kind of grace?

On the screen I watch the boy slide along the blacktop with the girl, hopping and twirling, their faces split to joy. They dance as if gravity is a suggestion they no longer require as they steal inside the hearse and coax the motor to roar to life. And the kids whose parents weep for their children's dead friends inside are the only ones who can see them, and they give chase like the Black boys who moments after I watch this video will appear as if from nowhere, like a cadre of ancestors, to flag down what is going to leave me behind. And on the screen the boy leans his head out of the window and he could be Slim or me or simply the moon finally finding its right sky as he grins. He and the girl grin, revving the hearse. If we are to be born running, I hope the road always rises for us; may we grin until we are a kind of forever, may 4eva be a mighty long time.

OLDIE

This is for the niggas in the suburbs and the white
kids with nigga friends who say the n-word.
—Tyler, the Creator

The first time I was ever called a nigger to my face I was "spared" the indignity of it being in English. Language will leave you grateful for the strangest things.

I was at a frat party wearing a voluminous white tee that I've owned since the eighth grade with the name and logo of every Negro League baseball team printed on the front. Dew dusted the roads in Swarthmore, October settled into the trees. In the dark, the trees were everywhere.

The man who called me a nigger was not a stranger—we were freshman-year roommates. The sound system boomed something bland feat. 2 Chainz. The first time I was ever called a nigger to my face the room was already vibrating, everything was already coming apart. The man who called me a nigger was freestyle rapping maybe the worst Faded White Boy verse in the history of Faded White Boy verses and rhymed my name with "mulignon." "Mulignon" translates to "eggplant" in Italian. Informally, it means "nigger," it means me.

I want to tell you "everything in me became a fist." The reality is that everything in me became a lens. I studied the party. I counted the white people in the basement (too many), I counted the Black people (we were both standing next to each other), I uncurled my hand.

I shoved my way through the sweaty white couples on the stairs and ran until I was out in the air. My white tee clung to me, heavy with other's people's sweat. I was alone staring into unpunctuated night, Black without witness. I'm not telling you this story for sympathy. I'm telling you how I first fell in love with the rap group Odd Future.

In 2012 I was the hapless manager of an equally hapless rap collective that was paid in pizza and exposure, in that order. Black and still boyish at nineteen, we rolled five, ten, twelve, fifteen deep across campus. Our songs were wack but that didn't really matter. Everywhere I looked, finally, we were legion. On a campus where Black people were talked about like ideas way more often than we were treated like people, there we were. I imagined that this was what it must be like to be famous, to never think of the word "consequence." This was what it must be like to be in love.

The real magic of Odd Future is that for some Black boys, we imagine heaven to be a place where we're the only danger to us. People called Odd Future's work "raw," but that's not what I heard. Folks said "raw" because we love lazy approximations for tenderness in America, we love the taste of the wrong word said confidently. What I heard when I listened to Odd Future was a way to fall in love with being unabashedly ugly.

Nobody in Odd Future wanted to be beautiful. They were ugly, and we were ugly, and this was how we were beautiful to each other. In the fall of 2012 my hair was dirty, my beard scraggly. It looked like a nigga hadn't seen the sun in days because I hadn't. I get ugly when I'm depressed. I didn't know I was depressed, I just thought I was ugly. And if I was going to have to be ugly all my life, I wanted to be ugly with somebody.

Tyler, the Creator, Odd Future's founder, wore short-sleeved button-downs with hand-drawn donuts on them. Earl Sweatshirt rapped about his bulbous lips while he swilled cough syrup and set fire to sheriff's whips. I wanted permission like that. The kind of permission only a friend who shares your ugly can give. I wanted to be so ugly it made me hyperbole: untouchable, loved by my niggas and only them.

Beauty, as we learned it, was for people with something to lose. I wanted to weaponize not giving a fuck. Our own collective moved across campus like bastardizations of another man's light, eager patrons of each other's flaws, and we called this love. And it was love, in the Odd Future way—fifteen boys who knew beauty not as a look, but a looking past. We grew fluent in each other, like boys do; we grew too fluent in looking past.

ii.

I'm high and I'm bi . . . Wait, I mean I'm straight.
—Frank Ocean

I didn't know—and I did—that I wanted to call boys beautiful in a whole other reckless way in 2012. But I couldn't imagine who could love me that way, if I was, indeed, that way. Being a teenager is mostly going to class and deciding what violences you can live through in the long term. I wasn't ever great at either.

The first time I heard Tyler, the Creator rap I was skipping class because I was "sick." This wasn't a lie, but it wasn't the whole truth. I told the professor I vomited because if you say you threw up nobody asks follow-up questions. Really, I just couldn't get out of bed. Depression thudded through my brain on a loop. It was more than sadness, it was a drumbeat, and there are few more pitiful lonelinesses than percussion in isolation. What I remember about listening to Tyler rap on Yonkers isn't the roach he ate, it's the way the blacks and whites seemed to pulse the same beat as my depression. That, and the way Tyler said "faggot," with the tenor of someone casting a curse they don't want to believe is already spoiling somewhere in their marrow.

When I was in middle school the only other Black boy in the class called me a faggot. It was casual, a flick of the wrist that I answered by blowing him a kiss. Then I learned that it was easier just to avoid being seen at all. I kept my sexuality a secret, even from myself. I didn't want to believe that when Tyler said "faggot," he could be calling out to me.

It goes like this often in boyhood, proximity and tenderness mistaken for each other. In summer 2012, I became infatuated with Frank Ocean and his song "Super Rich Kids." I didn't know, at first, that he was part of Odd Future. I worked at a job where I sat in a room with my headphones on, removing staples from the insurance files of long-dead people. I just wanted to hear Frank singing about the emptiness of rich folk. He seemed to know what I knew: the rich have no children, only sad assets.

Then I read about Ocean's sexuality. I watched the videos for "She" and "Oldie" and wondered what he was doing around so many people who claimed to love him, and maybe even did, but rapped as if they might shank his boyfriend. The real question was why was I doing the same?

Ignoring my own bisexuality, listening to most of Odd Future calling me out of my name, wasn't that difficult. I didn't need to do much to pretend it wasn't my name. Most of Odd Future's violence was so hyperbolic I could neglect the fact that to imagine a violence can also be a violence. My own collective, full of many niggas speaking with fear about "that gay shit," wasn't a knife to the throat, it was a subscription service: a tax I could forget I was paying until it cost me.

Our hapless group didn't have much of an endgame outside of the production of an album-length follow-up to a mediocre 2011 mixtape. I think, on some level, we were all invested in stasis. For some of the collective members from outside the college, as long as the album wasn't done there was still always a place to sleep, people who would find you useful and call it love. Others could continue to ride with folks who looked like us and pretend we didn't see the fucked-up ways we treated Black women. All of us could pretend we were home. So long as the album wasn't done, nobody needed to know what I was. I could be anyone, and if a white boy got out of line, fourteen sets of fists had my back. I wasn't willing to go back to my loneliness. Better, I thought, to be like Frank and have friends you must look past to love. Friends who said "faggot" to pull you closer, to say "you are like us, so long as you are our ugly, we will not let you pass into the dark."

iii.

And you don't even have to look 'cause we gleam
obscene in the light.
          —Mike G

There's a video that used to be on *Worldstar* of me rapping framed by too many trees and too many of my niggas. In the video, half the collective is in a semicircle freestyling to a simple beat, the kind that kids pound into lunch tables and coat their fists in spit trying to recreate with their mouths. I'm wearing a Captain America hoodie and calling myself "Renegade Patriot." You don't have as much judgment at nineteen as you think you do. It's the first warm day of spring and, in the cypher, we are jostling against each other. If you squint, you can see the Odd Future influence as we shove hard off each other; you can see the "Oldie" video. You can see how unsustainable it is to keep looking past. How if you speed the video up we almost look like enemies, if you slow it down we almost look like brothers.

The "Oldie" video isn't anything groundbreaking. The video has a messy, impromptu energy and some of the rappers don't even remember all of their verses well enough to lip-sync them. But there's still a magic there to me. The camera shies away as Tyler, the Creator's first verse starts to wind down and he all but drags the cameraman back towards him and his niggas, insisting he keep filming. I like to think it's Tyler insisting that he be seen, genuinely, among his people. Half of Odd Future flaunts Nerf guns and lightsabers and Earl Sweatshirt raps a sprawling verse in a button-down the same pattern as the Mississippi sky. I think about Tyler dragging the camera back. How he said, "You keep filming, fuck what they're saying." Like it or not, America, we're your sons too. We learned this ugly from you.

I used to tell myself that Odd Future's lyrics—the giddy way they could rap about the murder, rape and dismemberment of Black women and queer people—were intended to shock rather than terrorize. Like the Nerf guns: something shaped like violence but not actually meant to harm anyone. But what do you do when the odd future becomes the consistent present? Violence in America, and what we do to look past it so we can feel normal, sickens all of us even if we lack the power to inflict that violence directly. There is no such thing as "hyperbolic violence" in this country; there is only Tuesday.

What I wanted from Odd Future was to feel free. I wanted to be a nation's shame living a shameless life. What I got: proof that for all the ways I felt un-American, I still wanted to be. I wanted to stay sick because healing sounded lonely. But every lyric I mimicked was just further proof that the call was coming from inside the house.

Our collective was like Odd Future in a lot of ways, but maybe the most significant one is that no single event or big fight broke us apart; almost without a word we just grew in different directions. Today, I watched the "Oldie" video three consecutive times for the first time since I was a teenager and remembered how I felt when Tyler rapped, "I started an empire, I ain't even old enough to drink a fuckin' beer, I'm tipsy off this soda pop." And ain't it a blessing to have lived long enough for my friends to have seen multiple drafts of myself? I'm cautiously optimistic, in a world where Tyler, the Creator is openly gay but jokes about refusing to date Black men, that one day we might simply be beautiful to each other. Not all my niggas are my niggas anymore, but we shared each other's ugly for a while to learn the kind of beautiful we wanted to be.

The final moments of the "Oldie" video are as chaotic as you'd expect from a collective that used to regularly hurl sandwiches into the crowd. Tyler finishes lip-syncing his second verse, standing alone as the rest of Odd Future word-lessly files out of the frame. As soon as the last words are out of his mouth, he sprints and jumps with reckless joy into the mass of his friends. They spill onto the floor, howl with laughter, and it's easy to forget beauty can be as simple as this.

ZEKE'S COUSIN

Hands

The first time I'm mistaken for Dallas Cowboys running back Ezekiel Elliott, all I can think is, *Well, shit, I've been told I look like worse.* Over the years I've gotten Jordan Peele, Michael Jackson, The Weeknd, Drake and every Other Black Kid in Class I've known since the days we thought Gatorade could make us sweat blue. The man who'll one day be godfather to my children and I bonded first over being mistaken for each other seventeen times. None of the Black people I look like look like any of the other Black people I look like. But it doesn't matter, because tonight in Mississippi I'm in a bar called the Library with an anonymous white boy's hand on my shoulder, and this doesn't make it anything but another Saturday.

I figure a famous running back who actually looks enough like me that it can't *only* be racism isn't worth fuckin up a night I finessed my way past a $45 cover charge for. All my life has proven there's a thin line between honesty and finesse, tradition and side hustle. So I shake the white boy's hand to get him to stop touching me, I give him my fake name and go back to my drink. The bass is thick and the floor is clingy. I think about what it would be like if I was all the Black boys I'm supposed to be when the lights are low; trust me, we'd be packed one wall to the other, a whole parade of mistakes.

Since I moved to Mississippi in 2016, I've lost count of how many times I've had this talk. The one about who I look like, but ultimately am not. Sometimes it's funny, like that one time when a college kid, looking just like a malnourished Bob Costas, hurtled across the entire athletic center to ask for a selfie with me. A hand settles on my shoulder, and most times that hand is attached to a white boy I have never met and will never see again. I don't like to be touched by strangers, but it's already happening, and the question is already out of the boy's mouth by the time I look up.

"Hey, y'know who you look like?"

Over the years, I've settled into a lie. And I sell this lie by half rolling my eyes, as if I can't believe it's happening again. Then, very calmly, with full eye contact, I say:

"Yeah, that's my cousin."

Then I slide my hand into his, and before he even has a chance to disbelieve it we're dapping up, embracing, I'm congratulating the white boy for finding me. The thing is that I'm not Ezekiel Elliott's cousin. At least, not in any way I can prove. We're cousins the way all Black folks are maybe-cousins. I came to Mississippi to find the graves of my family, to find our records, the plantations that stood because of the work of our hands, to finally have a clear portrait of where we started and where we've been.

Every time I end up running this hustle I get the same result, a free drink. It's automatic, clockwork, routine. His hands, then my eyes, then my hands, and just like that I'm gone. I learned it watching Allen Iverson and Barry Sanders, I learned it watching my father; maybe we learned it from my great-grandfather, though neither of us ever met him. Either way, it's a good hustle: Hands, Eyes, Hands, Crossover, Gone. Just like that, with all the intimacy of a mirage. Maybe this is inheritance, how the white boy's hands mean "own" without him having to say it, how the men in my family all learned to vanish mid-sentence.

Eyes

The fortieth time I'm called Zeke, it is my first time opening my eyes in an hour. It is Halloween 2017 and beneath my barber cape I'm dressed in a pair of blue sweats and a slate-gray Ezekiel Elliott T-shirt jersey. The shirt is tight enough that I know I'll never order a "medium" in anything ever again. But that doesn't matter because I'm in Goolsby's barbershop on Jackson ave and there's no peace like knowing everyone in the building can fight.

I've been told I look dead when I get my hair cut. I can't blame folks—in the chair my eyes are closed and I sit still and generally don't speak unless I'm spoken to. It's a learned silence. I'm a Black boi who loves and kisses other Black

bois and in most barbershops this part of me is safest when
it's invisible. But not in Goolsby's, where I've had two bar-
bers who only ever call me Zeke. Two men I've loved like the
distant uncles they might be. Even the barber nigga who's
been waiting all three years I've known him for someone to
hop in his chair calls me Zeke. His job is to wait for someone
too desperate to be loyal, whose barber isn't working that day,
who's running forty-five minutes late off a lunch break, who
has job interviews and third dates, who has to pick someone
up at the glossy new-looking detention center right across
the street. And still, his chair stays dusty. I guess what I'm
saying is there's money to be made in the kind of trust that
comes with time. That there's a difference between being
called Zeke and being mistaken for Zeke.

The difference is in the fact I close my eyes the whole
time. When I was about seven or so, my parents took me
to a Wendy's a couple blocks away from our crib. I sat with
my back to the door and my fries in my hand like Wolverine
claws. A dude walked in looking like Chief Keef. Dude was
shirtless. It turns out he was also strapped and had a beef
nobody remembers with the assistant manager. And all of
this chaos was in full bloom by the time I turned around and
my father was hustling us out the side exit. Ever since then,
I only close my eyes around people I trust.

Goolsby's is one of the few places in Oxford's square where
Black people publicly congregate in the name of something
other than work. It was founded and is still owned by the first
Black alumnus in the history of the University of Mississippi:
James Meredith. Years have passed and still it is my barber,

my nigga, my shop when I'm telling anyone who's never seen the way its floor-to-ceiling windows chop the light into long clean lines, the way every humming blade sculpts the crowns of Black bois waiting to become Black men waiting to become beautiful.

And it is beautiful, the way Shaun's eyes are yellow at the edges like the beginning of a sunset; the way he says, "Zeke, lemme get finished with him and I'll be with you in fifteen." The way it always takes thirty, minimum, and it's cash only, so I walk down to the Regions Bank right below the most expensive bar in Oxford and I always end up giving Shaun whatever is in my pocket from the ATM. The way he has never said he loves me because he has never had to. The way I text him, *This Zeke, you in the shop tomorrow?* and how he opens it early just so I can look perfect at looking like somebody else. The way every time we dap and tip, he says "my man" or "my nigga" or "my Zeke" and I'm not owned, but I meet his eyes and it feels good to belong to somebody.

I learned that dap from my father, who still holds the title as the best liar in my family. In many ways, he went pro. For much of my childhood my father was considered a rising star in corporate America. A poet with writer's block but a god-tier code-switcher, my father loves a bar full of people he can charm. He's got a smoothness when he's flexing just how "articulate" he can be and it draws people to him. My father was the one who taught me how to code-switch, though he just called it "how to speak to white folks." Long before I was born, he got a hotel's presidential suite because the staff thought he was a different famous football player from the one strangers think I am. My father taught me that there's no sense in breaking any illusions white people have about you if those illusions can end in champagne.

Learning to code-switch felt like magic, until it didn't. I was uncoordinated as a kid and often picked near last for teams. Code-switching felt athletic, though, darting seamlessly between voices, between selves. It felt like my father was teaching me how to build a bridge from who I was to who they saw. In my mind he was a great athlete, not because he once swam in the Olympic trials, but because of the verbal duels I imagined him winning at work. Behind my closed eyes I saw him bobbing, weaving, spinning, getting around white folks trying to trip him up. He taught me white people were our opponents but that we could use their momentum against them. I watched him do this for years, a crossover that would've made Iverson weep.

And then, one day, it all went wrong. It went wrong because my father told the truth. A Susan from HR told my father that a mandatory training would be "difficult" and my father looked her right in the eyes and replied, "I'm a fifty-year-old Black man in America, what more could you possibly do to me?" He was gone not long after that. He still doesn't know why he said it. Like a freak injury ending a promising career. That's really all it takes.

And I think about that fifteen years later, strutting around the clinging fog over the town square in Oxford dressed as my maybe-cousin. A group of Black boys I don't know call out "Zeke" from across the street and I do his signature "feed Zeke" motion as a police horse trots past. I think about my father, about honesty, about the story of my great-grandfather's escape from Mississippi after his own lie finally failed him. The police horse snorts and the boys are already gone and I remember there are consequences to feeling too at home anywhere.

Hands

The fifty-seventh time I'm mistaken for Ezekiel Elliott, it is the night of my first bar fight. Of course, I don't know that yet. It's a Friday in Mississippi and so all the clubs are drunk with bass and it's wall to wall undergrads. It is nearly summer and the Library (the bar, not the campus building) is packed to the rafters with my students and kids who look like my students. They are sucking down Tide Pod–style frozen margaritas, singing along to threats I know they don't understand, their faces shining like the laminate on their fake IDs. And I'm not old, but I'm definitely too old for this shit. So I go somewhere else, to the Blind Pig, though I've gotten into the habit of calling it my bar.

The Blind Pig is one of those bars that you miss if you're not looking for it. It's two vast rooms covered with semi-ironic signs, three TVs playing one game, two TVs playing another and one playing a random Netflix Disney movie. Unless it's game day, in which case every TV in Oxford is doing pretty much the same thing. The walls are all wood—the same rich, buttery brown of a new set of Timbs. It's my favorite bar mostly because it's the only affordable bar in Oxford for adults. That and the fact the playlist is consistently fire but never blasting. I'm twenty-five at this point and any bar I have to shout to make myself heard in is a bar that I'll leave as soon as the check comes.

I'm outside the Pig chilling with the bouncer while my homie who's visiting this weekend gets another drink downstairs. We're watching the sky because it is full of unidentifiable pops, like fireworks but larger, sharper. It is as if someone is unloading a clip at the moon even though the moon is nowhere tonight. I ask the bouncer, Gary, if he thinks that this means there'll be a war. He pulls a shoulder-length hair back into his blond bun and shrugs. "Weird place for a war to start, but shit." I shrug as if I agree. I'm not sure I agree, but there's a strange hand on my shoulder, and a familiar question introduces me to the man who's about an hour away from punching me in the face.

His name is Memphis because he's from Memphis. He looks like if Randy from *My Name Is Earl* got really into *Sons of Anarchy* for a few months. He is tall with a thick, wheat-colored beard that's still patchy in places over his ruddy cheeks. He's accompanied by two other white boys and all of them are dressed like people who have multiple MMA decals on their trucks.

When he tells me his name, he says it just like that, with a smile on his face like this is a clever joke he's been telling for years. Of course, there's no way for me to know if it's his real name. And when I shrug off his questions about my famous not-cousin, there's no way for him to know if my name is my real name either. He grunts something that sounds like "pretty cool" and we both follow Gary the bouncer down the steps, Gary's man-bun bobbing behind him, a perfect blond circle like a full moon in October.

The Blind Pig has two rooms, one with pool tables and one without. In the room with the pool tables I'm teaching my visiting homie how to play darts when I hear another word that has passed for my name on occasion. One weird thing about being Black and constantly surrounded by white people who consider themselves "good" is that you can forget, just for a minute, that some white folks toss around the word "nigger" casually like they're returning a Frisbee. And Memphis and his buddies are in the corner right next to us, casually tossing the word. I think you see where I'm headed here. I'm told I slipped my glasses off and set them down on the table next to me. Maybe, even as I was telling Memphis not to say that word again in my bar, I saw where I was headed too.

There are consequences to Black dishonesty, and the trick is that they're nearly identical to the consequences for Black honesty. Memphis's fist arrives at my lip so fast I taste the blood before I see his eyes. They are proud eyes, hazel and glimmering as if he is telling the joke of his name all over again. I punch him in that joking eye. I leap into him and feel the second punch graze my cheek as I sink one fist and then another into his gut. This is my first bar fight, but it ain't my first fight. And all I know is that Memphis looks like the type of motherfucker you gotta put down fast and hard. I feel a third shot, directly to the ribs this time. I wheeze as I grapple for his chin, grab his teeth as if I'm planning to pull his jaw off its hinges, and push like the offensive lineman I once was until he is jammed into the corner of the room. I swing and swing until I'm lost in the music of his breath leaving his body.

And then I feel a pool cue across my arms. Every stranger in the pool room has come together and I'm being restrained with a stick, but the white boy who started the fight isn't. Memphis is wiping his mouth as his buddies check if he's all right, and already I can see him pleading his innocence—game recognize game, this is a hustle he knows well. Meanwhile a different stranger, a small white boy who could be anywhere from fourteen to twenty-two, is yipping directly in my ear, "You're better than him, you're better than him!" with the religious intensity of a chihuahua greeting a mailman. It'd almost be funny if I wasn't bleeding, but I am.

The next moments pass in a blur. My friend finds me. The bar staff, recognizing me as a regular customer, shepherd me to the back to give me a cup of ice to suck on to bring down the swelling. I spit one cube back in the cup and it's pink with my blood, a piece of rose quartz. We never see Memphis again because Gary kicked him and his friends out of the Pig. But not before Memphis could tell me he'd be waiting in the parking lot, in case I wanted to "settle this." I know this is a trap, but I'm still tempted.

The walk back to the car is a moonless Mississippi night. We parked at Goolsby's, so it's several blocks of walking while I spit bloody ice cubes onto the sidewalk. And my homie, who isn't Black but knows why I didn't want to wait for the cops, is telling me how sorry he is for not getting us out of there sooner. I'm thinking about my mother who made me promise I wouldn't die in Mississippi. How I almost broke the promise and so I've never told my mother this story. I spit one last ice cube onto the ground as we climb into the car. I try not to wonder if in the morning it will look more like water or blood.

Crossover

The fifty-eighth time I'm mistaken for Ezekiel Elliott, my lip is still swollen from the night before. I'm in a kid's bookstore, Square Books, Jr., window-shopping while the sun bullies the town square. It is the kind of weather you make a good memory out of. The bookseller asks if I know who I look like and I don't have the energy to run the hustle so I say, "My dad" and don't say another word. I've spent the morning on the phone with my advisor just to make sure the story of my first bar fight doesn't get out of control. After all, I came to Mississippi looking for the records of a story that also got out of control.

Here's the story I can't stop telling, what brought me to Mississippi, what makes me call it the Zero Country. Many men ago, my great-grandfather was an extremely light-skinned Black man from Water Valley, Mississippi. He moved to a town called Greenville, where he passed for white for a living. He sold insurance out of the back of a hardware store to make money to feed my grandmother, a baby who one day would be one of the prettiest girls in all East St. Louis. And then everything that was going to happen finally happened.

Reports conflict as to whether it was my grandmother, his wife or someone else who finally exposed him. The important thing is that someone or something did. As a result, a group of townspeople filed one by one into my great-grandfather's shop and told him he had twenty-four hours to pack up everything he owned. If he or anyone he loved was ever seen in the town limits again, they would be dipped in tar and covered with feathers. I'm only alive because two generations ago my great-grandfather wasn't murdered for not being what he looked like he was.

And isn't this always how it goes? There's a distance between who Black people are seen as and who we are. We see this happen every time we "fit the description," every time "you look just like," every time we are mistaken for someone else by Sally from Accounting who would've voted for Obama a third time but hasn't gotten our name right once in four years. We're expected to forget all of this, I'm expected to forget all of this. To forget that one time my great-grandfather told a lie and fled his home under threat of tar and feather, under threat of death by irony.

Gone

Nobody has called me Zeke in years. I guess every side hustle runs dry eventually. I left Mississippi in mid-2019, after graduation, but part of me is also still there. It is April, somewhere in Oxford there's a magnolia flower so heavy with petals that the bud can't sustain them all. Somewhere in Mississippi, a dozen petals come loose and drift to the ground and I wish they didn't look so much like feathers. Part of me belongs to Mississippi now. Part of me belongs to Big K.R.I.T. rattling my speakers, the catfish sandwich at Ajax diner, to Goolsby's, and this story I stopped telling about my famous maybe-cousin.

I wonder sometimes about whether part of my great-grand-father's story lives as a rumor in one of those Greenville families. If they talk about it, sometimes, in hushed voices. If they would ask me what I was doing in Mississippi and their eyes swell wide with recognition hearing about my side of the three generations between feather and mercy. Or maybe the violence of it was so unremarkable that nobody bothered to remember. I haven't decided which is worse.

What I know is that I come from a long line of Black folks who used dishonesty as a form of self-defense. This is my inheritance, the thin line between a tradition and a side hustle. My inheritance is men who were forced into being Americans in a country that, twice in my lifetime alone, has gone to full-scale war over a lie. America taught us to lie by teaching us that there is no reasoning with white supremacy; the Truth has no army, it cannot save you.

I inherited this story, I invented this particular hustle. I wonder if my great-grandfather had a routine just like mine when he swore he was white. Whether he tried it until it was clear that there was no preserving the life he had, that the only escape was to actually escape. How he ran until it was a kind of flight. I'm alone in a bar when I last think this. I'm watching highlights. Zeke leaps over a white linebacker. He is reaching out, Black boy mid-air with no wings. If you squint, you can almost convince yourself he's flying.

ME and ADONIS CREED ARE GETTING TOO OLD for THIS SHIT

1. Like boyhood, it begins in sirens—a dry klaxon baying in a hallway—it is Condition One, Code Blue, via the tracking shot, we are running even though we are seated; we are breathless when we see that a boy is beating another boy's ass. The boy below has a bruise that gleams like an alarm. This is how we meet the boy, who will become Adonis Creed. Without a word, we know that something inside him does not want to die. He is fluid, instinctive, like his father—right down to the sirens.

2. 2016 and lately, all my dreams begin in sirens. They end in sirens. I've had nothing but dreams of the police. In the right light, ya boi is Prometheus. Each night I watch *me* get

ripped away from *me*, then each morning I'm alive all over again. If I see a blue light, no matter the distance, I think, *What did I do?* I hear sirens even when there are no sirens, it is a sound that I am never without.

3. Even niggas who don't really know shit about Rocky know about the Rocky Steps.

4. In the summer of 2012 I knew almost nothing about Rocky, but I was brought to the Philadelphia Museum of Contemporary Art by a summer pre-law program. This was the first summer that my mind began, first quietly then all at once, to fight me from within.

5. There are seventy-two steps in the famous Rocky stairs and that day in 2012 was a perfect 77 degrees. The crisp white stairs of the museum glowed under the placid blue sky. Small children scurried upwards, legs chopping in place like the wings of new birds. Nobody said "depression" in my family. As a youngbul, everything I knew about depression came from black-and-white commercials where nobody was ever depressed once the sun came out. Lungs heaving at the top of the stairs, I started to wonder whether what I was feeling was more than my normal sad. That maybe this type of sad had a name I was afraid would swallow my own.

6. It's easy to say that I was running from something, so I won't.

7. I've never seen the Rocky statue without an accompanying line of people bouncing from heel to toe, waiting for a chance to take a selfie with the statue. Rocky is, for better or worse, a landmark like most American landmarks.

8. There's a famous comedy clip of Eddie Murphy doing an impression of Italians after they've seen *Rocky*. In the electric sheen of a purple-and-black jumpsuit that holds him close as a bruise, Murphy says the word "mulignon," which means "eggplant." Colloquially it means "nigger."

9. The joke is that Rocky will give a white boy all the delusions of grandeur he needs to come looking to get his ass beat.

10. There is no film in the seven-movie Rocky canon that doesn't involve a white boxer humbling or killing a Black opponent. An American monument, like any other American monument.

11. Ryan Coogler's *Creed* premiered in November of 2015. I was twenty-two and most of my dreams were about dying. In 2015 most of the Black people I saw on-screen were already dying. Or they were about to die. I'd been kicked out of college, and I lived in North Philly in an apartment that all summer had been home to approximately six niggas and one incredibly pissed-off dog more than the lease agreement allowed for.

12. There are months I try to remember where all I hear is the click of a pistol.

13. Off Broad Street in North Philly, I lived in the back room of an apartment where a squirrel had tried to make a home and found that sometimes home is a thing that can swallow you. The squirrel was trapped between the insulation and the outside world. It kept me up the whole night before arriving at one of my jobs and getting a call from one of my MFA programs to let me know my rejection would be arriving later that day. One day the noise stopped altogether. I needed a distraction from the Schrödinger's rodent situation in the roof, so I went to the movies.

14. *Creed* is a *Rocky* spin-off with a simple premise: Michael B. Jordan plays Adonis, the unacknowledged son of Apollo Creed, who died in the first twenty-five minutes of the first Rocky movie I'd ever seen. Adonis tries to make a name for himself in boxing by recruiting a semi-decrepit Rocky Balboa to teach him what his father couldn't. Like I said, simple.

15. Shortly before Adonis becomes "Donny," in the way Philly can very easily stretch your name into something like home, there's a scene that I love. In it, Adonis sits alone in a home theater, under footage of his father's legendary rematch with Rocky. The projector hiccups as Adonis rises with the melody of "Fighting Stronger," fists barreling through the air, his father briefly superimposed over him, Donny's shadow hustling to keep pace as horns swell beneath him.

16. Real ones know that there's more than one version of this track and in the shadow of his father, the music around Adonis is foreshadowing a remix featuring a Philly icon whose career had barely escaped the summer.

17. When the history of the *Creed* trilogy is written, we cannot forget that Meek Mill went the hell off on the first *Creed* soundtrack.

18. Friends, Romans, Jawns, I am once again returned from the summer to make an argument for "Dreams and Nightmares" as one of the few perfect songs of my lifetime. By which I mean to know Meek Mill's music is to know what about Philly made me fall in love with this city and thank it for every punch I learned to dodge.

19. "Dreams and Nightmares," the opening track of Meek's album of the same name, blooms in soft piano and from the very beginning it is clear it cannot stay there. In 2015 I often was stapled to my sweaty mattress by the shame of being the one left behind. The ascending keys of the piano open like calloused hands with a promise that Philly makes when you start to fall in love with it. Promise that what you see is not all there is or ever will be. Philly is a largely flat street city like the one I call home, but also a city that loves Rocky, loves the ones who learn to love the climb.

20. The whole of 2015 I will belt Meek's verse no matter how much depression has worn my voice thin, and the scorch

in my throat, the near empty of my lungs all will feel like I am alive in a city that does not want me to die. And then, the beat will fail momentarily like a heart, then surge out with Meek's voice nearly off the rails. Breathless, forever unfinished.

21. The whole next verse always takes me back to an insatiable July with me in the car hearing this verse for the first time, we spitting so hard we forget we need air. I think we may all pass out, we all may fade to black together.

22. From that Philly anthem, Meek spun many more in the shadow of that piano, that climb, an endless flight of stairs. Everything was heading upwards until it wasn't.

23. And so it was in the summer of 2015 that Meek Mill accused Drake of having a ghost writer and everything changed and Drake went from Professional Sensitive High School Boy to Extremely Buff Dominican Trainer Drake. And so it was that Meek made a couple of wonderful intros and one perfect one but rarely a project that slammed as hard as its beginning. And so it was that Meek didn't always know how to finish what he started. And so the summer rolled on with Drake dropping back-to-back diss tracks because Meek decided to start some shit on the road, that he meant to finish in the streets, and instead ended onstage at OVO Fest. Meek's brightness wavered, and I rotted in the apartment where the lights weren't always on but the couch was always full. And so it was a summer where nothing transformed into what it

was supposed to. And so the summer came to a close with all of us looking for a little more forgiveness than we found.

24. When the history of the *Creed* trilogy is written, we can never forget that we fall down, but we get up.

25. But we'll come back to that. I promise.

26. Carl Weathers's broad smile is blackened by the mouth-guard above each of his perfect bones and briefly, he could be my father. On-screen a boy shadowboxes in his father's light. I'm Adonis in a year where I barely remember that I have a face.

27. According to the homies, I have an annoyingly perfect memory. This is especially helpful in Philly because it isn't always grindtime; but it can always become grindtime, dickhead.

28. Flaming, bidding, the dozens. Whatever your city has called it, in Philly this is grindtime and it's announced as such, almost never by one voice but a choir that's about to tell you all the ways you done fucked up.

29. I'm not the most cutting dude when it comes to grindtime, mostly because even young as I was, I was still these teenagers' mentor and there's lines not to cross. But I do have a long memory, and if I am meeting you for the first time I'm looking you over. I'm observing, quietly, and I have a

couple observations tucked about you that I will whip out if provoked, without much of a second thought. Remember that day you tried to match one gray sock with one ashy ankle and thought no one noticed? I do, I ain't forget.

30. What I don't remember in nearly as vivid detail? All of 2015–16.

31. 2015–16 is a blurry loop of images of my every day, a training montage of the agony that, headed in to see *Creed*, I'd begun to wrestle into a kind of science.

32. My day typically began around 4:15-ish, which wasn't my choice. I would wake up from one of my police dreams to find that the morning hadn't even really begun. Now it was up to me to fight my way back to sleep but set six separate alarms within four minutes of each other titled, respectively: Wake Up, Wake Up (real), Get in Shower, Don't Play Yourself, Wake Up Now, Dawg. And my favorite: "The Bus Is Leaving."

33. I'd try to roll into the shower, the light pinked by the faded red paint of the bathroom. The fog that would get caught in your lungs if you weren't careful. Which brought on another panic attack and just like that I think you see how the whole year slurs together.

34. My college was in the idyllic, undistinguished suburbs at the end of the regional rail that spiderwebs out from

Philly. Once a week in the fall I had to take a train up to the college to meet with an academic counselor to explain how the viral and visible genocide of Black people was affecting my schoolwork. I can't really overstate the distance, not just mental but physical between one place and the other. If you've ever had a bus that if you miss it you're totally screwed, it's just like that.

35. Swarthmore College has many defining features but few draw the eye like the steps that cut a pearl-and-marble line down the central walk from the train station I nearly died at to the college that made me wish that I was dead.

36. I don't know how many steps Swarthmore College has. I could look it up. I won't.

37. Every week in the fall and every weekday of the spring that school year, I had to climb all too-gotdamn-many of those steps. And almost always at a college that had fewer than sixteen hundred people on its campus, I was recognized. Some well-intentioned person who I wasn't especially close to would come and ask me what I was doing "back so soon."

38. It's taken me exactly this long to internalize how often I had to return to the exact spot I stood on the train tracks the day of my almost-leap, my almost-death. It feels like no time has passed since then, that at any moment I can be thrown back down into that desperation. Back then I feared I had

lost my name and depression was a name too large for me to carry, these days I fear I lack the strength I had when I was closest to death. The stairs out of that year seem to stretch up and up forever. There is never enough distance between that hour and the one I am standing in. Each new day peeled back to reveal a day exactly like the one before it until it is all one uninterrupted take.

39. The first real fight in *Creed*, the name Creed never comes up—it is a battle between Donny, fighting under his birth name of Johnson, and Leo Sporino, the #8 ranked fighter in their weight class—it is also one uninterrupted 4:37 take, and at this point I think it's important to tell you that I think of my depression as a white boy in my head and that I cannot get out, so it's worth mentioning that Leo Sporino comes into it with the crowd on his side & I too have boxed in the brightest of lights and mostly begun with blood gilding my eye, a bruise fading to rose gold at the edges beneath my cheek & it's worth noting that I had a white boy student who looked a lot like Leo Sporino in a class I taught at one of the five spaces I was working at/teaching for in Philly and that this class was for youth who were on house arrest & Leo throws the first punch at Adonis Creed even though he doesn't have any real knowledge of who exactly he's fuckin with only that nothing has ever put him down on the canvas before & this is not the story of a student taking a swing at me at the end of a day where I'd taken two classes and then sprinted down the stairs to get on the 69 bus that picks up very few people from

the edge of Swarthmore campus and curls through acres
of suburb before dropping at the very end of the Market-
Frankford line which I rode all the way across the swollen
eye of Philadelphia to my third job—but it is the story of
a white boy who thought he could say "nigga" and tell the
judge who sentenced him to go fuck herself, because no
woman was ever going to tell him what to do—and it's worth
noting that the white boy looked a lot like Leo Sporino or a
roommate who I should have fought when I had the chance,
but didn't because I was afraid of being kicked out of college even though I only need this job because I was eventually kicked out and so maybe I should have at least gone
down swinging & Donny's bleeding on the screen by now, not
knowing this is the last night he will ever be Adonis Johnson,
as I'm reflecting on all of this—he's bleeding and losing the
fight until the exact moment that he isn't and I realize only
as Leo Sporino crumples to the mat that I haven't blinked in
four minutes and thirty-seven seconds.

40. The next morning Adonis is outed by ESPN and Sporino's triflin manager as the son of Adonis Creed. No matter
the stairs, no matter the running, no matter the father, eventually everyone must make peace with their name.

41. The battle between Meek and Drake was always a question of realness. Which is hilarious when you remember it
was also two grown men with pseudonyms writing mean poems about how the other didn't deserve to wear their name.

42. Donny says to Bianca, the love interest played by an underserved Tessa Thompson, that he's afraid of taking on the name and losing. I had my name, and I had lost more than I knew how to count while wearing it. I too was worried that I didn't have my father's strength, that I was ultimately a fake Randall.

43. I've experienced many shames in my brief life, and there aren't many that compare to feeling unworthy of being in my own family.

44. But we'll get back to that, I promise.

45. The year that *Creed* was released all twenty acting Oscar nominations were awarded to white actors. This would be the first of two consecutive years.

46. And even people like me, who never remember the Oscars until they've already happened, were pissed.

47. In the #OscarsSoWhite hashtag, begun by April Reign, folks pointed out that not only had it simply been a year with many good Black films and superb performances by Black actors, but that it had been a year of incredibly visible Black death. The Academy is out of touch with The Moment unless they are watching a Black person in extraordinary pain.

48. Many on Twitter agreed that Michael B. Jordan should have been nominated for *Creed*. And almost in real time, I

remember that this was one of the only movies that I'd seen all year, one of the only Black people I'd seen on-screen and never once expected to die.

49. I'mma keep it a bean, I am not arguing that Michael B. Jordan is a uniquely great actor, I don't actually think he would either. But I am arguing that he was, in fact, *Great* in *Creed*.

50. The debate about whether or not Michael B. Jordan could act wasn't baseless. In a number of his performances, there are simply times where he doesn't have an enormous amount of emotional range. The emotion wells behind his eyes but doesn't travel to his mouth. He has a tendency to say words at odd angles and while he's a very impressive fighter in *Creed*, nothing has been quite as bone chilling as hearing how his portrayal Killmonger says "Iraq" with about nine more *R*s than the word actually contains.

51. Much of the ongoing conversation on whether Michael B. Jordan can act tends to center around his relationship with *Creed*'s director Ryan Coogler, who also directed him in *Black Panther* and in his major motion picture debut, *Fruitvale Station*.

52. And yes, it's worth noting that *Creed* is the far superior film to its sequel, *Creed II*, and MBJ is significantly better in the original *Creed* which was a major contributor to The Discourse around whether he could act or was simply incredibly pretty and shirtless.

53. That being said, I tend to judge a performance by how memorable it was, whether it inspired in me a new way of living and there are two scenes especially in *Creed* that live rent free in my head.

54. The first is shortly after the low point in the hero's journey arc of the film. Rocky has cancer he won't get treatment for, Donny's girl Bianca (rightly) leaves him after he started a fight with the headliner of the biggest show that she's ever had a chance to do and he's been challenged to a clear stunt fight with "Pretty" Ricky Conlan, a dude who is both the heavyweight champion of the world and also about to go to prison for the rest of his prime for having a gun somewhere he legally was not supposed to have a gun. In conclusion, our boy Donny is down bad.

55. Of course, we know this will resolve because South Philly would riot if Rocky died of cancer. And the romance will knit itself together again because Tessa Thompson wouldn't just disappear before the third act of the movie even really begins.

56. But watching for the first time, I'm sitting in the Pearl Theatre off Broad Street, feeling much less certain that I know how to resolve what is happening to me. Not a moment goes by that I'm not in fear of a panic attack, my emotionally abusive first love was taking out most of their trauma on me, and every day I woke up in a country, this country.

57. This country that is, like all countries, a story that I could be written out of without a blink, I still can. At the end of this essay, that will not have changed.

58. The morning before my life began to change I discovered two things: (1) That the University of Mississippi MFA program was a perfect fit for me. (2) The University of Mississippi MFA program's application deadline had passed two weeks prior to me opening the website. Dread knocked me to the canvas again, throat closing as I silently sobbed and thought of how if I was just *better*, just more *capable*, my life would not be this endless climb. By the time the application was going to renew, I expected to be dead. What was the point of fighting? Why not stay in bed? Forget to eat and "forget" to eat until my anxieties outweighed me. I fall past featherweight until I weigh as much as the dark between the amber streetlights of North Philly.

59. But the trick to a great training sequence is to help the audience fall in love with the climb even if the destination at the top of the stairs is not promised.

60. And just like that we are in my other favorite scene in *Creed*. An homage to Rocky's whole hood running behind him as the dialogue of Donny and Rocky's reunion drains from the screen and we are brought back to the swelling music of "Fighting Stronger," an avalanche of drums as Donny Creed shadowboxes in Rocky's hospital room. The strings

glide underneath a choir that hums like the first full breath after a panic attack. And then, Meek Mill's voice arrives.

61. Meek Mill raps like many things including but not limited to a sped-up VCR. Someone who has missed their bus for an event they are already late for, and someone who is insisting that they are already on the highway for that same event knowing damn well that they're in the third quarter of a close game of 2K and will not be on their way for a minimum of fourteen minutes.

62. And on "Lord Knows/Fighting Stronger," Meek Mill raps like a prayer. Bold across the screen, Donny runs as now the song is struggling to keep pace with him and not the other way around. A bunch of kids from Frankford are a low din of motocross bikes as they holler at him to "make history, Creed" and all these Black boys, the ones I love and the one I am, are a flood of golden horses in the setting light and Michael B. Jordan is mostly yelling silently but I feel every word lost in the swelling of the chorus. I fall back in love with the climb, with this life that is mine. This life that I have had the strength to save before, and will again.

63. There's a popular self-deprecating joke at Swarthmore, that each class of four hundred people contains one Admissions Mistake. Now what exactly makes one an admissions mistake varies depending on the situation. Someone forgets to put water in their Easy Mac, twice, and now the whole dorm has to go outside for a fire drill? Admissions Mistake.

Forgot today was Tuesday because you've been up for nearly three days straight and now you missed the deadline you were gunning for the whole time? Admissions Mistake. Had a series of violent panic attacks from autoplay videos of Black people being gunned down that delayed your graduation by a full year? Well, you see the pattern here, don't you?

64. A month before *Creed* drops, I'm having an argument with my father about whether I really need a college degree. I tell him I don't know what it means if I don't make it to the other side. He says it means that he's wasted twenty years. I feel like the worst kind of mistake.

65. After eleven rounds of brutal blow by blow Michael B. Jordan's face has swollen to ruin, and still he begs Rocky that he has to let him finish. And in this moment, with no job, no degree and unsure if I could finish another hour of my life let alone the semester, briefly me and Donny become the same boy. At the core of Donny, his long and largely traumatic childhood before he came into his name, is the need to prove that he's not a mistake. Say what you will about Killmonger, Jordan's acting his ass off in that moment and I would burst into tears if I hadn't lost the ability to cry years prior.

66. And of course, he doesn't win. Adonis comes within seconds of upsetting "Pretty" Ricky Conlan but ultimately pulls up just shy, though he succeeds in knocking Conlan down for the first time in an undefeated career. He doesn't

win, sure, to set up the franchise and sequel and the sequel after that. But also because ultimately, it was never about winning, it was about falling back in love with that endless climb we just call living.

67. Over a plate of ribs I can't afford on a Friday night in New York, my life changes. My best friend, Nick, is the kind of person who notices you're sad before you do. And on this particular night I didn't realize how much I was still beating myself up over missing the deadline for University of Mississippi until Nick asked me what's wrong and didn't mistake my answer for the truth. I finally tell Nick that I missed the deadline and I'm all out of the fight I'd need to survive another year like the year we're in. And somehow, maybe ancestor or miracle, Nick convinces me to send an email asking to apply anyway. It feels improbable, impossible that I have any more miracles coming my way, but I'm wrong. Dr. Derrick Harriell looks at my email and emails me Saturday, trying to test whether I was arrogant, desperate or both, asks me to turn in every application material by Monday morning. I hustle, I make it to the top of the steps laid out in front of me and everything is in by Sunday morning. I'd been losing the fight until the exact moment I wasn't and without noticing had stepped into the rest of a life I hadn't expected to be able to keep surviving.

68. *Creed II* ends up falling short of the original for a number of reasons. The film largely takes a departure from Philly in favor of an LA setting that doesn't bring as much of the

Philly energy or *Rocky* history that makes *Creed* come alive as a long love letter to the city that birthed Rocky in the first place. Also the loss of Coogler as director often means that the incredibly talented Steven Caple Jr. is left to fill in the gaps of Coogler's brilliance, especially with close-form combat. And then of course there's the weird and fairly ableist plotline about Donny's struggles to love his daughter who is born deaf. Viktor Drago or no Viktor Drago, there's a bit more mess and uncertainty to everything.

69. But the one reason the sequel never quite coheres is that at its core this is a film about Donny coming to terms with the fact his life is no longer disposable to him in the way that it once was. Michael B. Jordan is significantly stiffer in *Creed II*, often looking a little bewildered to be in the sequel of his own life. He's begun, already, to be too old for all this shit. He has a daughter and a wife now, he's older than that boy with that dark moon of a bruise beneath his eye in *Creed*'s opening scene ever planned to be.

70. Up until the release of *Creed II*, Jordan had never played a character who didn't expect to die shortly after we met him. I had never seen him on-screen, dating back to when he was Wallace on *The Wire*, and not expected him to die. Yes, even in the final season of *Friday Night Lights*. And having lived a whole life longer than I expected to live, the confusion that swirls across his character's face is relatable as hell to me. He is older and more attached to his life than he has maybe ever been; neither of us know what to do with our hands.

71. I don't know that any of us get a clean narrative arc and I'm even more convinced none of us get a hero's journey. And yet by *Creed III*, Donny Creed is *definitely* too old for this shit, and says so at least twice, but Michael B. Jordan, both on-screen and behind the camera, has only matured in the role. Under his direction boxing matches are more traditionally shot, sporadic fight action than the lingering one-shot of Donny's first fight. The camera chooses instead to linger more often on his face. It feels like Jordan trusts that he can convey Donny at the end of his journey and inevitably on the road to one last fight that is halfway a straight-up boxing anime. During this final fight Donny and his long-lost brother and best friend, Damian, stare across the ring and see younger versions of themselves, brothers split by one night onto different paths neither expected to survive. Jordan trusts his physicality rather than his words to convey the almost unmistakable emotion of carrying the boy you were inside the man you now are. And at the end, he is the champion again, not because of the belt on his shoulder but for having maybe his last steps on camera be away from the ring, down from the steps before one last loving stare at his daughter, already pummeling the air like her daddy did beneath a projection of his daddy all those years ago. He shakes his head, an oldhead's smirk on our still-young lips. And I can live with that, alive and climbing still.

72. The final shot of *Creed* begins with a single step, Adonis helping Rocky up the steps that unofficially wear his name one last time. At the end, the two stand at the top of the

steps, staring out at Philly, a city that raised me up in its calloused voice and told me that I had more living to do, whether I liked it or not. By now, I'm getting too old for a lot of shit. But it's true what they say, at the top of the Rocky Steps you do feel like you can fly. After all seventy-two steps, I have climbed to the top of this essay—and against all odds, I can see my whole life from up here.

PUT ME ON

i. Put Me On: An Essay in 16 Bars

I'm not a rapper, but I used to be a bad one
Autobill cut my power in the night, call me Samson

Morning comes as the bleary smudge of sun slashing someone else's dorm room door in half and I cough myself awake.
I'm sleeping on someone else's floor because I don't feel safe
in my apartment. Because I have a meeting about getting
back into college in an office two floors below me that I can't
afford to be late to. I'm choked with dust and the sweatshirt
I slept in is too thin for January in Pennsylvania. I check my
phone and see that an autobill I forgot about has taken most
of my money. I don't get paid until next week. I have $32.67.

In the meeting I can't be late to I will have to beg a woman
for the opportunity to return to college, I will beg for the
privilege of being hurt again. I will go back to my apartment
and try not to think of everything I need. I will suffer to keep
this need private. After the meeting, I have to leave for my

job and then to my other job. If I can sneak onto the regional rail into Philly, today living will only cost $11.

Panic attacks have made me a morning person, or something like that. It's barely 6 a.m. and I'm already desperate. A couple of months have passed since my class graduated without me because I failed three classes. I failed three classes because there's a war going on outside, and we're losing. There's a war going on outside and videos of Black people being murdered are trending all up and down my timeline. There's a war going on outside and that makes me the kind of Black dude who gets panic attacks and passes out. I have a meeting downstairs in which I will insist I'm fine.

I am not fine, but I will say I am, because I'm twenty-two with no marketable job skills except the ability to tell people who are hurting me that I don't want them to leave me behind.

I'm twenty-two and I have a meeting downstairs with a white woman who will stare at me with practiced sympathy while I look back at her with practiced misdirection. I have $32, and a job, and another job, and lungs I can't count on to do their one job. It's 6 a.m. and I am texting my boss and my other boss to put me on so that I can make enough money to pay the train to carry me back to this same white woman next week so I can ask her to put me on so I can get my degree and never have to see this place again.

I believe everyone has a year they never really leave. I want you to feel the run-on sentence of the year that nearly

killed me. Eight months after the meeting with the white
woman, Donald Glover's Afro-surrealist siren song, *Atlanta*,
will premiere on FX. I will be in love, I will fall in love. I will
see the Black southern boyhood I flunked out of, I will be put
on to a story about hunger and who I could've been.

ii.

To tell the story I take it back another generation
Make sure you haters taste the history of my desperation

My father wasn't the only fifth grader who asked to be put on
in the summer of 1963, but he was one of the only ones who
heard "yes." I imagine him then, nine years removed from
Brown v. Board of Education, elbows shiny with Vaseline,
coming off his second city bus, having commuted from where
he lived in St. Louis to Walnut Park Center for the Gifted.
Walnut Park sat among a neighborhood's worth of towering
green trees and was surrounded by an exquisite iron metal
fence, each emerald-green post filed to a razor-sharp point.
I wonder if my father, staring at his newly integrated school,
noticed that what was pretty was also violent.

In the "FUBU" episode of *Atlanta*, a twelve-year-old version of Earn, the show's protagonist, lies awake hours before his alarm finally tells him it's time for school. I watch
Earn and see my father laying out crisp new clothes to prepare to leave far from home, to the land of white folks and

well-tended oaks. I see, when Earn stares at the gorgeous yellow FUBU jersey, what it means to want to shine, to be seen, to be the brightest thing in the room. To have planned the outfit all the way down to the socks. It's an American hunger, to want to shine so bad you'd bleed for it.

For the next few years gangs of white children make a game of chasing my father and other Black students home from Walnut Park. When they catch one of the students sometimes it's a beating, other times a cigarette lit and then extinguished on the arm. In response, the Black boys do old Black work; they adapt. My father learns how to sharpen the metal edges of a wooden ruler until it is crisp as any knife, how to jiggle the edge loose until the ruler is a switchblade.

I tell my father that a gang of white kids chases me around the playground every day. Their leader had said, "Every day you look so sad and I'm sick of it. You cry and complain about how alone you are, you should be grateful to be here. Not everybody gets to be here, you should be grateful to be alive. I'm going to keep hunting you down until you remember how lucky you are."

All my father wants to know is if they ever manage to catch me. Who can blame him? He was about my age when he learned how to keep his grief pristine. When he learned gratitude is a fist. How to dress so fresh nobody would suspect the ruler he alchemized into a switchblade, tucked into his socks. How to keep all your need hidden until you never needed white folks' money again. I learned to be the blade hidden in the ruler, I learned how to run.

iii.

Paper boi blowin smoke, three years a long year off
So step into my mind, lemme show you what it cost

I'm lying on my bed listening to a rat trapped in the ceiling of my apartment. The acoustics of being confined are unmistakable. Panic attacks and anniversaries have worn me down by twenty pounds and anywhere I go you meet my grief before you meet anything else. I send emails to professors who can't tell me from the other Black kids in class unless it's time to mark me absent. All the messages are long and eloquent in their desperation. This actually was a side hustle of mine, writing emails for students who were too depressed or too afraid of their professors to send them themselves. I'd make a couple dollars then I'd cram them into a vending machine. What I'm saying is, I've had a lot of practice writing letters that ultimately translate to "please."

Last semester, I wasn't allowed on campus for the sake of my "health," and this one I'm a full-time student working two jobs. If I didn't know everything I know about what white folks mean when they say "progress," I'd have been proud when they said I'd made progress. There is no progress, there's a room with a rat trapped in the ceiling. This year feels like it's been three. Above me something is itching its way to freedom.

Atlanta's gloomy come-up narrative centers on Earn, played by series creator Donald Glover. After discovering his cousin Alfred is an up-and-coming rapper under the name Paper Boi, Earn proposes he serve as Al's manager. Al pulls long and slow from the blunt in his hand before reminding Earn he has been out of Princeton for too much time for him to be trusted with both their lives—three years is a long year off. The show doesn't explain until season four what happened to Earn at Princeton, but I saw in him a similar lonely, an American loneliness. Behind his eyes, there is a year he struggles to talk about; this long year gone, this year we never leave.

All my life I'd counted on being smart, being good enough at school that I could make what doubted me feel sorry. But here I was reading math problems I barely understood by candlelight, since the power had been cut off in our apartment. I showered in barely warm water. None of this is baptism, none of this is romantic.

iv.

I had another voice way back in elementary
Here's another memory, a stone's throw from Emory

I'm a known Chicago supremacist but my first real memories are of Atlanta. They are of rising early with my father as we moved down our cul-de-sac to a little enclosure we called the Temple of Three Trees. I was energetic as a kid, talkative and curious about anything that wasn't nailed down. To make sure I wasn't singled out as a problem, my father ran me early in the morning. Sometimes we played games, sometimes we just ran for the sake of running.

The morning of my interview to get into the Atlanta International School passes like this. If I get in, we'll stay in Atlanta; if I don't, we'll probably move. I'm not old enough to know that this is an old myth, that school can save a Black family from anything. I'm not old enough to code-switch real smooth the way I will later in life. So my father is coaching me through some keywords that make me seem older and more polished than I am. He's teaching me the beginnings of my voice and the voice I can make it into. This is how I learn that the best place to hide your need is in your voice. The best place to hide your hunger is in your mouth,

Two out of ten of my favorite things about *Atlanta* involve the fact that it's a show about rap but literally no one raps. To the point that the camera sharply cuts away anytime someone is about to rap. Paper Boi's signature song, "Paper Boi," the one that will finally put the fam onto all the resources they've been denied by America, the one that will mean quick checks and no more trapping, the one that is mostly his name and some vibes but will mean the death of need, is not rapped by Brian Tyree Henry. It's rapped by Stephen Glover, whose voice is noticeably higher. In the pilot, before everything goes left, Alfred confides to Earn that he has quietly always hated the song the way Kanye hates "Gold Digger." And I get it, I know what it is to be put on by a voice that is not yours but says your name repeatedly.

By every available metric, I bombed the interview to get into the Atlanta International School. I took a rock from the ground outside the building to give to my father as a souvenir of the loneliness we were trying to opt into. The rock looked like any of the other hundreds of rocks, but this one felt like it was mine until it didn't. A teacher ripped it out of my hands, shoved it in his pocket, claiming that I was "messing with the landscape." I don't think I used any of the keywords my dad taught me on the drive over when I asked what made him act that way.

I showed the wrong skill and never was in line to be a southern Black boy after that. I showed that I could steal a petty thing. I didn't prove I could go unnoticed. I didn't ask why we needed to be put on at all, why we were asking so desperately to be lonely.

v.

DuBois ask, How does it feel to be treated like a problem
Got a couple chains in the crib, how's it feel to wear all of 'em?

In the ninth grade I was a very underwhelming but enthusiastic rapper called "Decibull." I dreamed of buying my parents a house they never asked for and other things that I'd watched child prodigies do to support the people who were supposed to be supporting them.

The problem was, I was very bad at rapping. I had a single with exactly seventeen views on YouTube, but that didn't stop me from updating the Chicago section of the Wikipedia article on rap with my name, for the exposure. Years have passed and still I've never seen Wikipedia delete some shit so fast. So I know what it's like to want to be known more than anything else, to think of being known as a kind of currency, especially when you don't have any actual currency.

When I was a rapper, I was a Black boy who was beginning to look more like a Black man, but could never be mistaken for a Black man unless you hear "Black" as a synonym for "problem." Paper Boi was once a Black boy named Alfred who was treated like a problem. Years later, Paper Boi is in a bar and the bartender asks to be put on; he presumes he knows Paper Boi because he's seen him on TV. What's the distance between being seen and being known? I'm not always sure, but I know Paper Boi's grimace because it's my father's scowl. It's the look of someone once treated like a problem and now like a resource, a door to be walked through. It is the exhaustion, the old Black work, of picking the "right" person to push the family forward. It's my family's one ugly heirloom.

The rapper is so often the archetype of the hungry provider, someone who no longer needs very much but is surrounded by need. We play this need on the corner, in the car, we talk on how this need began because we come from Americans who come from Americans who come from Americans who never asked to be Americans but found themself beneath a belligerent sun in a place like Mississippi. My father never wanted to be a rich man, just to muzzle loneliness long enough to make hunger a blue and distant memory.

vi.

Bougie niggas got put on, flexin all the wages
Why so sad walking around with them blue faces?

Far back as I can remember, me and bougie Black folks have
never gotten along. It's nothing personal. I too love *The Fresh
Prince of Bel-Air*. But it's been twenty-seven years now of me
and every Great Value Carlton Banks having beef basically
on sight and I know a pattern when I see one. I'm ready to go
through however many days I have left on this earth accept-
ing that I will never be someone folks are thrilled to have at
a Juneteenth party.

The joke of the "Juneteenth" episode of *Atlanta* is that
nobody likes their bougie cousins unless they're an even
bougier cousin. Or the joke is that all the Black girls are
draped in blue. Or the joke is Black capitalism. Or the joke
is celebrating the anniversary of white folks' lies collapsing
around them. Or the joke is that freedom is something you
can be put on to. Or the joke is the master's tools dismantling
the party. Or the joke is the blue sheen of new money. Or
the joke is that money can save you from the lonely of this
country. So I guess I was right, the joke was Black capitalism
all along.

I look at the party on-screen and see all the Black folks I
went to college with. Taking selfies in a building that used to
be a stop on the Underground Railroad. I see myself caption-
ing a picture, dressed in the fanciest clothes I could scrape
together from H&M's sales rack, "The New Black Elite." I

see myself, feeling like I made it even while I was miserable. I never wanted to ask where I'd made it to. I see our messy pride at being treated like some of the chosen ones, those "excellent" Black folks who'd gotten somewhere white folks never wanted or expected us to. I wondered why the way we talked about our love and our pride always had to be tied to something white folks wouldn't allow. I wondered what happens when Black folks who felt they had to be excellent their entire lives were faced with the reality when the realization sets in that nobody should have to be excellent to be free. Gradually, I felt bluer until I stopped being in photos at all.

I didn't want to spend the rest of my life doing the Jack and Jill acrobatics of people who think going to college is the same thing as a personality. The mansion in the "Juneteenth" episode of *Atlanta* strikes me every time I see it. Sure, because it's beautiful, but also that it could easily pass as a building at my college. The trees and sprawling grass, that suburban quiet that can only be bought.

I know what it feels like for Van, *Atlanta*'s wildly underserved female lead, to stand in that house asking to be put on because she has no job, nowhere else to go. One year before the premiere of the "Juneteenth" episode I will take the train up to the college that kicked me out right before my graduation. I will stand and grin next to my then partner as if we are still dating. We are not still dating. It is the inauguration of Swarthmore's first Black president and I've been invited to read a poem and give a speech introducing her. I will smile, I will dress up, I will be excellent even as I feel like I am dying. It will be my quiet way of asking to be put on again, to ask without asking not to be left behind. That night I will introduce myself with a miserable résumé, I will try to distinguish myself. We will talk about the Underground Railroad, about freedom, about history, about excellence. Three days later this president will reject my request for financial aid for my final semester. As of today I am still paying for it. What I'm saying is I look at Van in that house, surrounded yet alone and I get it. I know what it's like to grow to resent the kind of beauty white folks pay for, that it mocks you after a while, the indignity of standing in someone else's heaven.

There's a lot of ways to ask to be put on and many of them involve saying nothing at all about your need. In the "Juneteenth" episode Van wears a thin periwinkle dress while the Black lady who owns the house, Monique, wears a blue gown she might have snatched from Michelle Obama's giveaway pile. And there on the walls, two Margaret Bowland paintings, the white woman's hand exploring the majesty that is any Black girl's face. The Black girls on canvas staring defiantly out from beneath masks of blue paint. The episode, like the paintings, asks how triumphant we can be from behind our masks, behind the ways America feeds on Black need, on the moments we can barely stand to look each other in the eye.

This is what I mean when I say American Loneliness: we understand that to need is to risk being let go. The poet Claudia Rankine, who titled one of her books *Don't Let Me Be Lonely,* tells an interviewer from the *Spectacle* magazine: "To say, 'don't let me be lonely' is to say, 'don't ask me to exist in a position that allows for my own annihilation.'" In "Champagne Papi," another *Atlanta* episode, a dude with a pizza and a mixtape begs Van and her girlfriends, "Put me on, please, please, don't put me out." The rapper's face is a flicker, there and desperate and then gone just as quickly, as if even the camera is shamed by his need. And it doesn't only affect Black folks, just look at Craig.

Craig is Monique's husband in the "Juneteenth" episode. He is the kind of white man who does slam poetry. He's the type of white man with a decanter of Hennessy and several framed pictures of Black people tolerating him with their mouths wrenched into something like joy. And of course the joke is that white people who do slam poetry often get put on for their ability to make Black people sit through their guilt. And the joke is that all of those Black folks secretly wish they would keep that shit for the open mic portion of their family reunions. And the joke is that it's a white man screaming, "Jim Crow is haunting me" repeatedly. The real punch line being that you don't need to go much further than woke white kid Twitter to hear the same thing, and you don't have to go much farther than America for them to prove it to you.

The final shot of "Juneteenth" is of Earn and Van parked at the side of a road having car sex in front of some woods. I wonder sometimes when I watch the episode if Van is thinking of the question she asked Monique, about whether she was sorry that she couldn't have both understanding and intimacy. The question about what it costs to be put on. I wonder if she noticed Monique never really answered, but paraphrased Ntozake Shange. How it is redundant to be both Black and sorry in the world. I wonder if the answer would have made Monique feel too lonely, too blue.

Here's a story no one knows: Once, in junior year of college, I was scheduled to read a new poem I'd written to Donald Glover. It would be one of the first times I'd ever rapped in public. The few friends I had at school continued their yearlong project of ignoring my depression because of how much it reminded them of what it was like to be lonely. Still, these were my niggas, and the only place I felt understood was in the arms of these boys I would call my brothers because we were lonely in the same place. I walked out into the rain at 3 a.m. while they were in the main lounge of our dorm, just to see if anyone would get curious about where I was disappearing to when everything had been closed for hours. Nobody did. I kept walking until I was in the woods around Swarthmore, in the thin, sopping branches.

I walked until I was deep enough that I figured campus security wasn't finna come if they heard a lonely nigga screaming. And then that's what I did, I screamed. I walked in the blue light of those spindly woods, cursing at God until I fell and twisted an ankle, then I limped back out of the forest because I don't know any good stories about sad Black people in the woods. I don't look at my own face often, but that night I must have been blue as a Margaret Bowland painting, blue as an American Lonely. I hoped on my way out of the woods that at least our blues remember us.

vii.

Squad the only cure for an American lonely
This one goes out to all the token homies

I was always a lonely child, but I was also never alone. No matter where my family moved, me and two of the other Black boys in school would find each other like magnets. One time we all ran for student council on a joint Black Liberation ticket that called for reparations to be paid anytime we got mistaken for each other. We lost, by a lot. Still, our almost-love was how I learned The Nod, a way to say "squad" without ever opening my mouth. When I see Earn and Al and Darius, I see us. We knew each other by our parents' weary palms along our shoulders. We knew exaggerated laughs and "proper" grammar, but above all we knew those hands; subtle anchors as if, untouched, we might disappear.

In the last episode of season two of *Atlanta*, "Crabs in a Barrel," Earn is on the verge of being fired by Paper Boi for being a generally unreliable manager. Paper Boi's best friend, Darius, tells Earn something I've been hearing all my life: "Y'all both Black so y'all can't both afford to fail." I've heard this sentence so many times across the years, but the first time I heard it, I heard it in my father's voice. On-screen the two Black boys living in terror inside the bodies of Black men are looking at each other and it is the Blackest need. One boy without the space to hold the other. One's eyes saying, *Touch me please, fam, I could die of this loneliness*; the other cousin's eyes responding, *I love you, but so could I.*

Me and the other Black kids at school always knew the stakes. We knew this was the plan for survival, we knew this was the best gift our parents could afford. We were all our lives governed by the worry of being kicked out. We never knew when this opportunity our parents had pinned us to might be taken back from us, so we almost never spoke of our need outside of song lyric, outside of metaphor. We loved each other as best we could in our American loneliness. This was how I learned that intimacy and solidarity were not the same thing. We were told to lift as we climbed and when/if that failed we were taught to let go and blame gravity.

viii.

I got some grief that's led me to the wrong conclusion
Woods go on forever, lord forgive me all of my delusion

When I first got to Mississippi, I didn't really rock with nature. I'm a city kid to the core, also there's no love lost between me and bugs. Nobody has ever gotten me to use the words "hike" and "fun" in the same sentence and I'm not old but I'm too old to think that will ever change. All this to say that I never expected to fall in love with Mississippi's woods at the end of the hardest year of my life, but I did. After graduation, after I moved out of the room in my Philly apartment, after Dr. Derrick Harriell looked at my Hail

Mary application to the master of fine arts program at the University of Mississippi and bet on me to be better than the story my grades told about me, I pulled up to Mississippi in 90 degree heat, feeling, finally, like I had a chance. Against all odds, I'd been put on.

The woods that surrounded where I lived in Oxford are flanked by pines and kudzu. That first year in Mississippi I lived alone. Most nights, I sat on my camping chair on my little balcony, staring off into those woods and telling myself stories about the wildest things I could imagine living in that forest. And then, Mississippi would send something stranger. Stray dogs rumored to be the children of dogs displaced by Katrina sometimes file out from the woods to kick it near the dumpster I lived across from. I think about this and the yawn of the branches of a dogwood tree, how the petals ride the breeze until every street around us wears a pink, sequined gown. 2015 had taught me to crave quiet, Oxford taught me how to fall in love with a different kind of noise. Of course, not every sound in the woods is an invitation; we're still in America after all.

The episode "Woods" follows Paper Boi on the anniversary of his mother's death; he's the victim of an attempted robbery, which forces him to sprint into the woods. Just like that, another fugitive from his own grief. A Black boy living in terror inside the body of a Black man all alone in the woods. And isn't that one of the most American lonelinesses you've ever heard? The woods in the South are not the woods in Walnut Park, or Swarthmore, or even like the trees I ran between in Atlanta so many years before. Seven people were lynched in Oxford, Mississippi, and nobody has ever told me which tree.

Paper Boi runs into a man who may actually be a hallucination. All that's clear is the glare off the box cutter the man holds to Paper Boi's throat. How clear he says, "Keep standing still, you're gone, boy . . . The only people who have time are dead." I see all our shared lonely from here, how you can spend a lifetime with your grief keeping you company and emerge as alone as before. The only way out is through.

Still, the morning of Halloween 2020, hours before I will make a second trip through the woods just outside of Water Valley, Mississippi, the town where my family was once enslaved, I'm in a different woods. It is early morning and the bleary smudge of the sun slices the basketball court in half. Tucked in the backwoods off Jackson ave, I'm shirtless with the thickest beard and longest hair I've ever had. Truly, COVID had me looking like Corbin Bleu's ain't shit cousin. I will always be a Black boi who comes from need, from a long line of Black men who dreamed of ending our hunger by hiding in school until we could invent somewhere it was safe to be ourselves.

I still think everybody has a year they never really leave. I also think Mississippi taught me the way back to the present. To this moment, with a ball in my hands and some free time before I return to trying to find my dead. I shoot my shot and watch its perfect arc. I remember that the first thing I fell in love with about Mississippi is that there's so much sky here.

There's no romance to the story of my escape from Pennsylvania to Mississippi, my "reverse migration," as some

people call it while they ask me what I'm doing in Mississippi and I tell an old story about a place where the light
flinches with memory. But it feels like love to be back and
alone, that for once my loneliness is not more important to
me than my solitude. It feels like love to be listening to the
woods yawning, imagining, singing under the gold barrel of
the sun. It feels like love to think of everyone and everything
that carried me out of that year. It feels like love, it feels like
the whole forest humming *we on, we on, we on.*

BLACK DUDE
DIES FIRST

Dusk in Mississippi and the wind bends the branches above my head into a tragicomic moan. The sun pulls low along Jackson ave as I walk home from another missed bus. Sometimes in Oxford I blink and the twilight goes with it, the sun's warmth gone as if it were never there. I guess we are all lonely in the season that widows everything, even the trees drowning in the kudzu which strangles the branches without ever making a sound.

Night is fragile in Oxford.

The dewy quiet of the road home has few streetlights to its name. None of the dark here is metaphor. None of the quiet is peace.

The quiet is, however, occasionally torn by the engine of a massive pickup truck. You know the type, huge *Mad Max* wheels and a "Yeti Coolers" bumper sticker. That pre-pre-pre-midlife crisis apocalypse-mobile that gets polished to a suburban clean. That truck you fill to the brim with boys who could be killers or senators with the same hands.

Every once in a while one of these trucks whips past and I hear their laughter, hungry and overlapping before I hear the engine roar forward. And I don't know much about horror movies, but I know plenty about terror. And the moon is reflected in the hood of the truck in the instant between me whipping off my headphones and the yelp from the truck that is maybe a slur, maybe a joke, maybe a hotty toddy, maybe a threat, maybe a laugh that dies in the air between us as the boys zip away, the wind free moving through their identical haircuts.

Beneath the moon, I'm only a couple steps from home; only a couple months and miles from me leaving Mississippi and two months later three students I could have TA'd for shooting Emmett Till's memorial for sport. There's a graveyard I always forget about on my walk home. The bared branches shiver and moan above me again and I suppose the Jordan Peele interview I watched earlier that day made a point: the difference between comedy and horror is the music.

⧬

THERE'S NO MUSIC to begin Jordan Peele's third film, *Nope*, a thriller that followed up his award-winning comedy partnership, *Key & Peele*, and his two seminal horror ventures, *US* in 2019 and his debut film *Get Out*.

Instead of music, there's disembodied laughter that comes in waves to some cavity-inducing punch lines for a fake sit-com called *Gordy's Home*, whose titular star is a chimp that is about to brutally kill most of the cast as the laughter turns on a dime to cries for help. The point is the spectacle, the way our eyes are unmistakably drawn to the uncanny image of a slipper standing on its point, a single drop of blood against the blue canvas like the flag of a long-forgotten country.

Nope is about many things, aliens, legacy, spectacle and how satisfying it would be to watch someone who works for TMZ get swallowed by a giant parachute-shaped apex pred-ator nicknamed "Jean Jacket." Y'know, Americana. And it is also, at its core, a film about two Black siblings, the many-times-over great-grandchildren of the first Black man ever captured on film, whose father dies exactly five minutes and twenty seconds into a movie. Now, to try and get money to save their ranch and the horses they have looked after and trained for generations these two Black people are looking to capture undeniable video evidence of the alien that has been chewing up whole stadiums of tourists. *Nope* premiered two summers deep into the pandemic, two siblings up against an enemy as wide as the sky trying to bridge the gap between what they experience and what they know the world will be-lieve. And what's Blacker than that?

The last normal day of 2020 was bright as an omen on my street in Minneapolis. After grad school I'd been taken on for a job in publishing and I was on my way to the venue to celebrate a friend's book release when I saw that a weird ac-ronym of letters, COVID, was spreading like, well, a plague.

At that point all I really knew about COVID was that Rudy Gobert had it and that the man they made president seemed confident it would blow over in a couple of days. Which of course meant it was a lie. It meant our enemy was as wide as the sky, it meant there was no negotiating with what wishes you dead.

It was March and whole cities' worth of doors shut.

It was March and the whole block went silent.

It was March and it would end in two weeks. It was March and niggas got in fistfights over months' worth of toilet paper.

It was March and the tragedy already felt like it had stretched for years.

It was March and every mouth disappeared.

It was March, nobody knew the rules.

It was March and it has sort of stayed March forever.

In April nobody knew what to wear to the apocalypse. The grass grew wild where we couldn't stand and if you saw someone on the street you awkwardly leapt six feet away from them. In April, COVID was the worst group project we ever failed, the worst game of freeze tag ever. In April I lost my job and any superlatives that may have once been associated with me died on the vine.

In May everyone was really into *Tiger King*. In May the country has an appetite for spectacle. In May the rich are their own country. In May hardly anyone's my president these days. In May anti-vaxxers licked locked doors in protest. In May everyone was catching up on *The Sopranos* and taking master classes for what they'd do in the new world. It was May and the difference between horror and comedy is the music. It was May, there had never been so much silence. It was May and George Floyd was murdered by the police on a street corner in Minneapolis and the new world was the old world all along.

The thing about the alien invasion narrative is that it often counts on the idea that in the face of an existential threat to global society, we will all go full *Independence Day* and rally towards a big win over the invaders.

But then the pandemic came along and—I cannot emphasize this enough—niggas was coming to blows over toilet paper and whether germs were even a real thing. It was and still is the world in which my phone was flooded with snippets of a video of George Floyd's last breaths. I have never made myself watch the video. I never will. I have seen enough videos of the last minutes of a man slowly being murdered by an officer, who knew him and who would have been granted the authority to kill him even if he didn't, to know that there is no negotiating with what wants you dead.

In the days that follow Floyd's forced departure from this world, the sky is heavy with smoke and sirens. The Target I used burns to the ground and the police station it collaborated with burns too.

I dipped to Chicago to look at apartments because I had no job and if it was finna be the end of the world I wanted to at least go out in my own city, laughing under my own sky.

When I came back, there were soldiers outside the doors of my apartment building. I adjusted what passed for a mask over my nose and mouth and climbed the stairs into my ashy shoebox of an apartment to wait for a Grubhub order.

I watched the twilight settle over the national guardsmen, laughing unmasked at a joke that dies in the air between us. I blink, just as the sun sets on their rifles.

৪৯

MID-PANDEMIC AND LIVING is a choice that I can't seem to stop making.

The hours slither past and most of what makes one day different from another is the echoes of my neighbors in the hallway, the thudding steps of the toddler who lives upstairs, the weed smoke curling up from the vent below.

We are all in this together.

We are all in love with the word "us."

Every other sentence begins with "Since." We are all looking back. Some of us with love. Since the pandemic began, I say "after" all the time, and I've never known less about what I mean. This was the pre-vaccine world, the smoke was still on the air. I'd go out for my silly little walks once or twice a day while new things went missing.

We are all in this together.

We are all "us."

We are all going to beat this thing, and then forget because we are Americans and this is our trade.

Since the air had turned to lava, most days found me against my will becoming intimately acquainted with my next door neighbors' sex playlist. A truly terrible sex playlist made up of Ja Rule and the eight saddest Whitney Houston songs in existence. There is no after. Since that sex playlist started around 9 a.m. and closed around 1 a.m., my headphones were always in. I tried to drown out the sound of someone else drowning out the world while I wiped the edges of various packages with Clorox wipes.

We were all Americans. We are all in this together.

Since George Floyd was murdered, I've taken to walking the streets at night with a bat over my shoulders. The president is saying "after," again, like most words he says—I have no reason to believe that he knows what it means.

We were all in this together.

We were all Americans.

Every sound was too close. When the last moans of "I Have Nothing" would fade from my neighbors' speakers, I would remember I had a different problem. I had a mouse, trapped somewhere in my walls, again, and that lil mofucka was triggering the hell out of me. It was 2020 and murder was televised. It was 2015 and murder was televised. It was America, only some of the living could laugh.

Since George Floyd was murdered, white supremacists tried to firebomb the building across my street in the middle of the night. Since we were all trapped, we almost became an "us." It had never been easier to die, and still I couldn't choose it.

We were all Americans.

We are all in this "after" together.

While America is a film about race, *Us* is not. Peele's second film instead is about the debt of unprocessed trauma. It's as much a slasher as a true horror as the film begins with the declaration that there are miles upon miles of tunnels beneath America, and in this world some of those tunnels are home to exact clones of each person created to control folks like puppets, called the Tethered. We're first introduced to this concept when Addy, a silent film disguised as a Black girl in a "Thriller" T-shirt, wanders into a house of mirrors and finds herself eye to eye with her Tethered who seizes her by the throat as thunder roils above.

Eventually, these Tethered beings rise up from the bowels of these pipes draped in red with gold scissors in hand to slay their above-ground counterparts. When asked who they are, a wheezing Red gives a marrow-chilling chuckle. She knows what we know. They are Americans. There is always a nation beneath the nation we are standing on. What is faced may slit your throat, what is ignored will slit your throat with a smile.

Since the rules of America are the same as a horror movie, I stayed inside rewatching *BoJack Horseman* and talking about the nation and what can be survived. At the end of *Us*, with Red successfully slain we realize through her whistled song that she was the original Addy all along. What has haunted her for all these years has not been the Tethered Addy escaping a world of raw rabbit and endless hallways. It was that they always could have gone together back into the boardwalk. Instead, they were American girls, and there could only be one. We see the final shot of Addy and her traumatized bloody family climbing into the back of an ambulance and driving off through the California foothills as columns of smoke billow up and form a nation of their own on top of America. The Tethereds join hands.

Sometimes, describing the "after" of the pandemic feels a bit like this closing shot.

Peele loves to compose an ending where the big unspoken joke is that all the characters must fight for their lives for a broken prize: to keep living in America.

The joke, the horror, is that to some degree there is no after.

And trauma, too, can be a bit like this. There will be no complete "after" to the pandemic. No matter how hard we forget.

From the confines of that studio in Minneapolis, the itching in the walls only grew louder as I tried to bury the noise of still being alive. Living was a choice, yet it had never been easier to make it look like an accident if I stopped. When there wasn't Ja Rule, or the slam of an arguing couple's door there was faintly, at the edge of my hearing, the sound of a train arriving. A train that is never late, but never arrives either. I am always a little bit back at those train tracks, where there is no after. I'd shove in my headphones and shuffle some Big K.R.I.T. and the gold of that perfect weather for dying would dim and melt into a set of grills.

I missed the stretch of that sky, I missed my old world.

The yawn of the train tracks became the moan of every tree I passed under in Mississippi.

Seven people were lynched in the county where Oxford and Water Valley are.

Once you know that, none of the trees have the luxury to be metaphors.

What goes unsaid in the ending of *Us* is that the Wilsons have won and they are doomed for winning.

What is their "after" in a nation that wanted them dead and is now half dead itself?

⚘

DUSK IN CHICAGO and I promise all the trees laugh like Black boys in the end.

The trees above my favorite spot in my hood all lean away from each other like old friends about to scatter at a joke, their gnarled brown hands spread wide as if they mean to embrace the entire breeze.

Oh, to end like this: the wind whistle high as any song threading the distance between terror and humor. The trees hold so many alternate endings—yet bloom, still, as the dark passes over them.

The question of how many different ways *Get Out* could have ended was what first told me that this was a horror movie that was not mostly trafficking in Black terror.

I didn't see the movie in theaters mostly because I'd spent a whole year, a whole life, watching the Black dude die first.

I was in no rush to double down on the shit. But of course, reports began to trickle out; not just from the horror movie homies but from all along the internet. Wherever my data has been shared without my knowledge or real understanding, there were people discussing what was The Real Ending.

Canonically, the first imagined and shot ending of *Get Out* hinges on the fact that Chris, the photographer protagonist meeting his illuminati brain surgeon in-laws for the first time, could have ended many times before the story actually ends. The whole of *Get Out* is steeped in a suburban, Connecticut smoke screen. Every white man in the movie is a knife, every white woman is generationally talented at pretending they're not also in on the act. Y'know, Obama presidency c. season one.

At the time, much of America was working fiercely to forget the many violent reasons there had never been a Black president before. The word "post-racial" got invented, and everything has been downhill ever since.

Peele wanted to show that even if you do manage to unearth a generations-long white supremacist cult stealing the bodies of Black people, summarily kill every member of that cult and stop the practice forever, you're still Black. You're still a consequence of an argument you were born into. And so, after all of that, the blue-and-red glow bathes Chris's face as the last light fades from his white girlfriend's eyes while she smirks. Chris is, in Peele's eyes, not the sacrificial lamb but a kind of martyr. He has escaped the prison that his in-laws sought to make his body, only to end up in a different prison for the crime of loving and saving Black people.

In this way, he is one of the most relatable protagonists of all time.

But as video upon video of the police murdering Black people circulated, Peele revised. It wasn't necessary to remind his audience that the Black dude could die first, or second or a hundred times before breakfast without anyone batting an eye. He didn't need to remind us we were fragile, he needed to make us laugh and believe that this one time things could be different. There's a quality in Black laughter that is as much about mental escape as physical. When I'm laughing with my niggas, we are always running, and never in the same direction. We are holding each other, even as the space between us grows, yawns wide as the mouth of a tree. And let me tell you, the true ending of *Get Out* will always inspire that kind of running.

There is no after, there is no alternate. There is only the lights of the siren blooming hyacinth and dahlias across Chris's face. There is only his best friend, Rod, the one person who would have believed all he has seen and known, stepping out from the lights. Because he is T-S-Motherfuckin-A.

Even years later, even after the pandemic began, I feel the laughter build at all my alternate endings, branching tragicomic before me.

It could have all ended generations ago.

It could have ended when the first hand realized the tint of my great-grandfather.

It could have ended in Greenville.

It could have ended where the pistol has been a kind of pollen.

It could have ended with my grandmother and it could have ended with my father.

It could have ended on the train tracks, in the officer's car, at the protest over what definitely happened in the officer's car.

It could have happened in my dorm room and it could have ended on the train that is always coming in my mind but never arrives.

It could have ended in the pandemic, I could have ended it and the death count would have risen like a whisper.

I have housed innumerable unnamed tragedies.

I am a palace of alternate endings, and yet, there is only one path forward. Back to Mississippi, back to the magnolia trees and the dogwood branches, back to the sweltering arms of my dead.

I wanted to forget, not just the pandemic but what I'd left unfinished in the Mississippi I'd left. I had never found the graves, the archives, I had been counting on this search to take up so much more of my life before the smoke began building its own country. I realized I had been counting on my life to continue for the first time in years, and I was ashamed to be so late to my living.

Had I really tried everything I could to see those archives, face Greenville and the earliest place it could have all ended?

Had I wasted the last years on a long trauma response I didn't have the will to end?

How could I have not seen the tragicomic punch line coming a mile away?

Red smile, red country, red hands wrapped around my throat.

How could I have forgotten that "apocalypse" also means "revelation"? The sun set beyond my tiny window, filthy with smoke.

I look up in Chicago, dusk slipping through my fingers under the resurrecting trees.

It is 2020, it is the dusk of America. All my dead are waiting for me. Because there is no alternate, there is no after beneath our undeniably American sky. Someone and then another someone and another asks me for a book rec about racism so they can learn retroactively that I have known they've been racist for a long time. I swear; all the trees, all the trees are laughing.

Classic me, finally learning to breathe just in time for the rules of breathing to change and the rules of America to stay almost exactly the same.

It'd be a good joke if it wasn't killing me.

OAK RIDGE
BLACK CEMETERY

Normally, I don't get down for this kind of white people shit, but here I am, on Halloween, kneeling alone before a maybe-stranger's grave. It is October 2020 in Mississippi, there is no sun for miles. I've spent three years in this state looking for the graves of my family members, who were once enslaved near this town. The town is called Water Valley and there are two cemeteries for exactly the reason you think. The sky is gray, a light fog clings to everything while I keep doing the type of shit that gets white people killed in horror movies. In Mississippi, weather bridges the space between a plea and a prayer.

Five years earlier, on a day in June 2015, the weather was perfect. I was standing at a train station in Pennsylvania deciding whether or not to kill myself. I had just been told that my final semester college grades were so bad that I was barred from returning to school. The sun bore down across the campus in thick gold ropes. A year of videos of police shootings on autoplay paired with the shame of watching my senior class graduate without me had finally pushed me too far. I saw the train coming and I wanted to leap, I wanted to die. Or I wanted to stop living. I'm not always sure what the difference is.

In 2015 I felt like every choice had been taken away from me; I wanted my death, at least, to be mine. But you know I didn't jump that day.

Three months later, I learned the violent story of how my family left Mississippi during the Great Migration. Some days, the hope of finding my relatives' graves is all that keeps me on this earth. Searching for proof that they were here once keeps my brain from wandering back to that train, that perfect weather for dying. Everything is green, lush, perfect as the grass above headstones.

The weather in northern Mississippi is a petty architecture even on its best days. Halloween is not one of its best days. Still, in October 2020 I have driven hundreds of miles because Halloween is my favorite holiday and because I think this time I'm equipped, finally, to find my great-grandmother's headstone. I am twenty-seven, kneeling in a segregated cemetery on the outskirts of Water Valley. I run my hands along graves so faded they have almost ceased to be graves. Tombstones are cracked at odd angles and moss curdles where the letters should be. Some are overrun with cactus; every amnesia blooms into something that draws blood.

This Halloween I'm not only breaking my "no graveyards" rule, but also my rule about not doing group costumes. Me

and the homies are all supposed to be dressed up as characters from *The Good Place. The Good Place* is a show where
a group of humans die and find out they're each other's hell.
I wander around the Oak Ridge Black Cemetery and find
none of the names I've come looking for. I think about how
there's a Good Place and a Bad Place, and I wonder if there's
a name for the loneliness of none of your kin being able to
find your body.

I think mostly in movie quotes and song lyrics. I rarely saw
myself in pop culture; every TV screen was a locked door,
an eye that refused to see me. Every breath I take in Mississippi reminds me that I come from people who were enslaved
a handful of miles from this graveyard. I close my eyes when I
feel the letters of the graves, touch another headstone that has
fractured like a bad tooth. *Wheelis, Curry, Leland.* I mumble
as if the soil can answer, but it's just the trees sounding like
the city clerk who gave me the cemetery address asking what
I'm doing in Mississippi and me rolling my eyes to say I'm
looking for a man who was briefly every phase of the moon.
Wheelis, Curry, Leland. All the names of my family members
before we were Randalls, all the graves I cannot find. I beg the
graves like I do the weather. *Sing back, sing back, sing back.*

All of Water Valley's records were lost in a fire that missed
my great-grandfather by a month, having already left with
his wife to start a new life in Greenville, Mississippi. Sometimes it feels as though Mississippi was as eager to forget
us as we were to forget Mississippi. So we are nowhere, my
family is a rumor—a ghost story so common America never
invented a name for it.

It is 2020 and there is an election in a few days and for the hundreds of miles between my home in Chicago and Water Valley, I have seen thousands of Trump banners. I am aware that neither candidate has ever wished me well. Nothing in this country ever has. America is a gaping mouth with an insatiable appetite for Black suffering, Black labor, Black cool, Black flex, Black silence, Black death.

What I'm saying is that Oak Ridge is a segregated cemetery at the edges of a town that once suffered an immense fire, and both the first spark and a whole country are responsible for that. The needle of a cactus skips over the fabric of my jeans as I kneel at another grave. *Wheelis, Curry, Leland.* I feel the edge of a letter X and move to the next memorial. Kudzu shuffles Mississippi's best green dress over my head, my fingers stumbling through the aftermath of a century's hard rain. I learn all over again: it will take a miracle to find the graves I'm looking for, and there is no time for miracles.

Wheelis, Curry, Leland.

I hum their names, a little rosary of the forgotten. I swipe the red mud from my knees. I beg and it is no prayer at all. *Sing back.* The dead don't need reminding, but the living are always desperate for a song.

And then at the edge of hearing, a name. Beyond the rain, my best friend calling me in, he is knelt at the edge of a hill half the graveyard away. He has found something and all my blood has leapt in his direction. Something is happening in my body. Something I have only felt at the state line of Mississippi. I can feel my legs beneath me, I am running heavy with rain towards where Noel is pointing to the ground. And I am thinking now, of the earlier rain, the one that greeted me at the Mississippi state line two days ago and the "Welcome to Mississippi" sign that tells me this is the Zero Country, home of the Blues and without meaning to I am pressing harder on the pedal. I always want to greet Mississippi with a roar—with a sound so huge that no fear could survive inside it. It happens, every time, me at the wheel negotiating the dark beyond my headlights as the pistons below me push forward like an answered prayer. And maybe that prayer is also my own, that I need to believe my gone are as eager to be found as I am to let the engine sing into the ground, *I have fallen but I have not died; I've given my name to this reverse migration, I have come back for you after all this time.*

My legs have borne me up the hill, and I am nearly there. Rain in my eyes, rusted mud falling from my jeans in sheets. It is the right lighting for a kind of resurrection. Oh my long and beautiful dead, I have come to what was made your home and I am pulled towards you by hundreds of horses, if not thousands. I am the chariot, the iced-out whip roaring past the cotton fields. And in my running, curses unspool for miles around. In the cotton field nearby, without a single song, every boll of cotton floats upward—hangs in the air until the cotton mocks the stars. I am inches from the grave now—my gorgeous gone, perhaps laid in this cemetery because even certain parts of death are Whites Only. What of the squirrel's skull at the edge of everything, flayed bone-white by a crown of maggots? Have the flies in this town always answered every iridescent hunger? In the escalating rain, at the edge of the grave Noel is pointing to, for the first time I can notice I am afraid of what comes in answering a generational thirst.

I wondered how I had been pulled to my gone by what feels like a thousand horses, but was I ready? For the end? If I don't have the gravity of the unanswered to pull me forward, what keeps me from the next train? The next sun, the next uninterrupted field? I'd ask the trees but they only ask what brought me to Mississippi. I'd ask the kudzu but it only asks what kind of ghost story I've become all these miles from home. I'd ask the rain, but the grave only says "Curry." No first name in the marble, no first name in the dirt, no names anywhere on the sheet of the buried curled in my fist and pulped by the drizzle.

I kneel at the grave and feel a stranger's grief, a long groan curdles to a scream before becoming a sad wordless song. In the rawness of my throat, I say their names and only the kudzu answers.

I wanted to die, or I wanted not to live anymore, or I wanted to be among my dead. I'm not always sure what the distance is.

TELL the HOMIES I'M in the AUTUMN and THEY AIN'T GOT HOODS

1. I imagine death like a passing of leaves. At twelve I'd never seen the lights of the Vegas Strip, but I remember that when I learned Tupac Shakur bled out on a street in Las Vegas, I had a clear vision of a death I never witnessed. I imagined the pavement yellowed and blood unfurling a scarlet so deep it's basically black. I imagined blood that changes by circumstance, imagined this was what Tupac knew about time.

I don't remember wanting to die at age thirteen, but I know that I did. What I remember is I had a Makaveli-branded jacket with Tupac's face superimposed across my shoulders. His head knelt in almost prayer, fingers quivering near the bridge of his nose. I'd sit on the L and think of how Tupac saw his own autumn approaching. His work on "Thugz Mansion" told me he may have known autumn as I've always known it, a complex heaven of scarlet over yellow, death disguised as the changing of leaves.

2. The white boy leading the protest looked like Asher Roth had fallen on hard times. He said familiar things, so we let him rock. I say "we" though, even now, I don't think I believe that there was a "we" in the Shadow Lounge in 2015. If there was a we, we were something sad, but not unfamiliar, which is maybe the worst species of grief. Nearly everyone I love has encountered a summer where grief became an obligation.

Asher Roth Protest Leader was trying to hype up the crowd as he skittered frantic across the stage listing enough grievances the protest was about that it felt like more of an injustice potluck with some poems thrown in. I tuned out, thought of what it feels like to have no fight left, and wondered if I was there. Across the street, the sun refracted off one of the few windows nested in a parched Oakland building. The purple of that light fell across my skin and I wondered if there was anything Blacker than exhaustion.

3. I don't know if I know any Black people who have wanted, truly, to be alive the whole time they've been alive. I was taught early and often the terrible rarity of Black folks dying of old age. In my family, we do not discuss what it is to struggle with suicidal ideation, even when it is spring; even when rain vibrates through the dirt and everything that has color insists *alive, alive, alive.* We pronounce it "selfish." I have

a habit of saying "survival" as if it is the only song I know, some days it is. Most people I love say *How much longer* with their voices, with their eyes, with the yawn of their exhausted bones but only the wind answers.

4. I don't fully remember the first time I told a room of my students that the eighteenth-century British poet John Keats and Tupac were essentially the same dude. But, I am correct—they were. What I remember is that there was a thing I didn't say, but I'll say it to you now: until the day I turned twenty-eight, I spent every birthday of my twenties thinking of a Black man who died at the same age. Tupac and Keats both died at the age of twenty-five, one by gunshot on some real American shit and the other by tuberculosis on some real Oregon Trail shit. Ultimately, in my experience, a man is a body wrapped around a question. And the question of Tupac's and Keats's work was always what to make of being young and alive, when young is all you imagine you will ever be.

I felt the question sing to me, its whistle high and piercing as a train that is always arriving in my mind.

5. And look, it's always worth mentioning the suburbs have no addresses in the dark—and that shit is by design.

Everything in the town of Swarthmore is built with the idea that you've been there your whole life, that this is a comfortable darkness between streetlights. The bulbs flicker into an autumn of a kind, and it can be beautiful if you fuck with not knowing where you are. If the dark doesn't demand an answer of what a kid like you is doing in one of the richest suburbs in all of Pennsylvania and you know it's not a question your student ID can answer. If you know that no answer will be sufficient. In that flickering light, yellowed and thin as an accusation, I was making my way to the only Target for miles in the summer of 2014. I was listening to Tupac through some dingy Sears headphones that only fully worked on one side. I wish I had better motivation, but to keep it real I was hungry and everything else was closed. The almost-rain clung to the air like a veil, and even knowing where this memory ends, I still want it to be beautiful, that moment before the memory becomes significant, before the moment snaps shut clean as a trap.

The thing about the Target outside Swarthmore is that it is surrounded by the Springfield Mall. In 2014 it was proudly home to a Ruby Tuesday's, a Sephora, the Sears from which I had gotten these mostly broken headphones on clearance and pretty much nothing else. Oh, there was also a GameStop, my bad. Anyway, the Springfield Mall was always easy to spot because as you walked the crooked smile of broken pavement, the parking lot lights shined a blue halo into the clingy mist above. And ya boi had that pain, that violin in my hip, playing that same note it had been for four to five years.

And on this particular night, Tupac's voice faded in and out of focus in those cheap-ass headphones. And there's a way, even in the early August of it all, that the chorus of "Thugz Mansion" harmonized with the leaves that had already fallen. And I was tired, and hungry, and a nigga had never been so happy to see a Target—or so devastated to see that while Target was absolutely supposed to be open, the mall had closed. Which meant I'd come all that way for nothing. So I sat a spell on the bench of the bus stop, hoping the driver was Black since they were generally down to let me ride back for free if the bus was empty.

And then this older white woman sits down at the other end of the bench.

The next song flickered in the right ear of my busted headphones, so I half hear the opening piano of *"Runnin'"* before I realize that she's talking to me, and just as the Edward Snow hook whines in with "I wonder if they'll laugh when I . . ." I pause the track. And at first, things are as fine as they can be. I am good at smiling when I don't mean to and the musty mouthed woman is chattering about Target being closed too early, and like any other night in America shit is cool until it's not.

"Excuse me, young man, are you Black?" cuts through my quiet headphones.

Before I can answer, or point to the bright blue dashiki I was wearing as an answer, Bus Stop Lady has already continued on with:

"Now there's no need to get offended . . ."

I move to say I am not offended, even though I am, because I'm a boy doing an impression of a man, doing an impression of a man doing an impression of a man trying desperately not to get killed.

But again, Bus Stop Lady was still going, milky eyes glazed and staring over my head as if she was talking to a ghost. All her threat slurred through the gaps in her casual smile, one long yellowing sentence unspooled into the fading summer.

"I'm just asking if you're Black because there was a Black lady here earlier, she got offended and I told her, 'Now you look here, you don't talk to me that way—I am white, do you hear me, and you are Black and you just don't talk to me that way or I'll call the police, this, this, this, this, this is America and Black people they don't, they don't, they don't—don't live here, they just die here.'"

I'm sure the night was warm, because I remember the cling of the dashiki's cotton to my chest. But in the phone call I faked, the sprint I did not hide away from one woman who wanted me dead into the suburbia that agreed, it tasted like the first notes of autumn were already on the August wind. As I sprinted, the pain in my hip yanked into melody and I could still hear Tupac's "Runnin'" crackling in the bad speaker, ". . . if they'll laugh when I am dead." Before the quiet returned and I was the only sound for what felt like a whole season. Autumn in the static, autumn in the failing streetlights, autumn in the suffocated leaves, autumn in the swelling of my knees. My people, my people, our perpetual autumn; what insufficient heavens we have been offered.

A day later I posted a Facebook status on what I experienced, a few days later Mike Brown was murdered. All of autumn dims, and my father and I have our first and last conversation on whether I have been feeling suicidal. I say no, I say I am fine, I say I am not going anywhere. Even with him, I am sometimes good at smiling when I do not mean to. I am at the window of the library later that semester, the elegiac hum of a Tupac song under my tongue while I sit through a November meeting about a group project I don't give a shit about because the grand jury verdict comes down tonight. I am the only Black kid in the group, certain seasons are never late. The grand jury agrees that there is no victim and there is no crime and my classmates are sad, but resume their meeting. It is autumn, I am remembering that my favorite song is about a heaven I'm afraid to qualify for—I close my eyes, blood pounds in my ears and all the leaves abandon their branches.

6. Keats's poem "To Autumn" is one of the most famous of his odes. Of all Keats's odes, it's maybe the most consumed with his growing understanding that he was not long for this world. In the first stanza Keats describes a good harvest, autumn's bounty delivered just prior to the winter, writing, "To bend with apples the moss'd cottage-trees, / And fill all fruit with ripeness to the core; / . . . Until they think warm days will never cease."

7. In some of my memories, the summer of 2015 was so hot I watched the walls of my Philly apartment slowly bow and melt. It was the summer of too many shootings, which is to say it was an American summer. But the warm days, I knew, were bound to wither into memory, scatter like leaves as autumn arrived. My will to live became a bouquet I forgot the occasion for. Maybe this is true for everyone, I only know that it is true for me.

That wrestling all my life with a part of my brain that simply doesn't want to be here any longer, that's the song I know—I wrote all the words and I'm still writing them now. That I struggle to explain that it is not always a matter of the desire to die, it is that living feels as unsustainable as I know that it is. I didn't expect to live much further past twenty-two because, well, I didn't. I don't want to pretty this, so I won't. There are days that I cannot stand in place for more than five minutes without beginning to feel my knees swelling in protest. There's mornings I wake up and the torn place in my hip says that I cannot move for hours.

I love my life, and yet.

Living is a season, an autumn that wrings the color from the year. When I am feeling like I can't stay alive, when I hear the train calling still all these years later, it's more about "Can I do forty more years of not being able to stand without searing pain?" I had not expected to pass through this autumn so many times, and the idea that there are more ahead—a whole bouquet of years that I forget sometimes I have ahead of me. I don't always know how to accept that this life, I want to pretty this; but the season has passed me by again.

8. Tupac Amaru Shakur died by gunshot at the beginning of autumn on September 13, 1996, at the age of twenty-five. Like Keats, a lot of the trajectory of Tupac's popularity is owed to his own mortality, the posthumous releases, prominent among these being "Thugz Mansion." The Anthony Hamilton 7 Remix is a slight deep cut from Tupac's 2002

posthumous offering "Better Dayz." The track itself is a kind of autumn. We find Tupac, like Keats, contemplating what may lie beyond his short, doomed and beautiful life. "Ain't no heaven for a thug nigga," grunts Tupac, matter-of-factly, and it is as if he has already seen beyond summer's promise. I listened to this at fourteen and felt that Tupac knew what I knew, warm days cease, the winter comes and it is the implied silence at the end of Keats, at the end of everything.

9. In "Thugz Mansion," Tupac begins his first verse with "A place to spend my quiet nights, time to unwind / So much pressure in this life of mine, I cry at times / I once contemplated suicide and would of tried / But when I held that 9, all I could see was my momma's eyes." And it comes at the tail end of describing a heaven built not out of trumpets but bass, not out of clouds but from the arms of one's brothers. Heaven is a promise to the weary that nobody can prove has been kept. Still, Tupac wants above anything on "Thugz Mansion" to envision shelter and mean it, and that's the core, isn't it? At the end of elegy, we build the house from each other.

Tupac was always masterful at this, the elegiac ode, capturing the both-and of a life that he became increasingly obsessed with the ending of after being shot the first time. It is part of what fed both his and Keats's posthumous genius. And it is where my mind was when I began writing what became my first book. In the dregs of that summer of 2015, I began writing a book that I didn't expect to see the end of.

The book is called *Refuse* because, like my name, its sharpness is a matter of the light that holds it. In one mouth, it means trash, disposed, undone; in another it is the fingers pushing aside the bayonet, that part of me that thrashes itself to autumn trying to stay alive.

10. Keats opens the final stanza of "To Autumn" with "Where are the songs of Spring? Ay, where are they?" It is the only mention of spring in the poem and the question is rhetorical, but I've got my theories. As I packed the last of my belongings into a suitcase and moved back home to Chicago for the first time since I was just a kid in an oversized Tupac jacket, spring 2020 was, like heaven, a question of who sings the hook.

Maybe you know it, maybe you've only heard of it and maybe you never have but the hood got a spring all its own. My neighborhood was flourishing into that spring as Lori Lightfoot raised bridges and shut down trains to keep the streets' grief at a reasonable volume.

And there's a way this can be an essay about Short Disagreeable Police-Loving Niggas Who Need a New Barber; but I'd rather tell you about a rusted-out Toyota at the end of my block. Out west, around my way, yellowed grass feathered out from cracked pavement and a chill clung to the light as I shivered and sucked Mild sauce off my fingertips and tried to get the lay of everything. It's the false spring in Chicago that'll trip you up every time if you let it. The bared branches, the blackened snow that clings to the block like plaque, even in the most golden of light nothing trusts itself to be alive again yet. But at the end of the block, all alone in the yellowed grass, I saw a 2002 Toyota Camry. It had been abandoned, the grass grown high and wild around it, its windshield caved in by a brick, one mirror entirely lost and the back seat sequined by crushed glass.

And my first thought, looking at this Bush-era hooptie was *Honestly, same.*

But as I looked closer, the wheel wells were threaded with stalks and stalks of lavender. Lavender through the cracked rims, a bouquet over the headlights, purple heads curling into the jagged edges of the back window. I forget sometimes, the west side has flowers for days and never where you expect them, and that's a kind of spring. I know there's a metaphor in there about redemption but maybe heaven can be a place that asks less about redemption than reimagining, than repair, than finding the lavender amidst the wreckage.

One thing about "Thugz Mansion" being a posthumous release is that there's some debate about which of the three versions of the song best captures the vision Tupac had for it. Spring is a matter of who sings the hook, the hook is a matter of how we find harmony with the dead.

The original version of "Thugz Mansion" is entirely acoustic, only a plucked guitar and Tupac's vocals shade in the vision of a heaven made only for the imperfect. The 7 Remix does all of this but pairs with a sweeping production score that crescendos with the way only a young Anthony Hamilton can caramelize a note. Hamilton confided in an interview once that the track took him roughly an hour to find the space to tell of this chromed-out mansion in the sky. This is generally the version I've preferred since I was a kid. But one spring evening, sitting at the top of my steps with the sun pulling low along the block I say, "God, I love the west side" and a stampede of three-wheelers roar and chitter down the block, their neon lights iridescent as cicada wings. "God, I love the west side," and a warm breeze answers. The whole hood got a spring all our own and we ain't got to share the lavender of it with anyone. And just like that, the original "Thugz Mansion" hook plays in the shuffle and I remember that spring is a matter of who sings the hook. And oh, my niggas, haven't we been sung so wrong?

We are the kind of hood where we know every blue light, every yawp of siren is for us. We are overgrown and messy, some of our windows fanged by where the brick entered and no one came to clear it. And still, J. Phoenix is right, that in every corner of every hood, there's a spot where living is a little easy. It doesn't take much to make a heaven, it turns out, it doesn't take much to make a spring.

And so again, it is spring in the hood and the lavender wreaths that same Toyota that was never hauled away. We make gardens of the forgotten, even and maybe especially when we are the forgotten. At the corner store, I dap an OG and admire the autumn color of the tiny bottle of Hennessy he tips back. Indeed, maybe there is no heaven for a thug nigga. Maybe there is no spring awaiting any of us; maybe we live our whole lives as metaphors and all our deaths as rhetorical questions. Maybe. But maybe also, heaven can be a barbershop in the setting of spring. Me and all these old-heads sitting around watching *The Last Dance*, their crisp caesars faded to ash, our jaws nearly unhinged with laughter. And all of us uncles and cousins for this hour, and all of us "thugs" when the blue lights siren over the neighborhood, and all of us weary and west side and all of us the lavender threading the rust. Music is thawing from every speaker that thuds by and we build this spring on that harmony between the light and the dead.

Heaven, like the hood, is many things—I hope it's this as well.

GREENVILLE

When my father was a child in St. Louis, Mississippi was a threat aging Black parents made to their misbehaving, silver-toothed children. Threat to send them to relatives and cousins, to family friends and grandparents, to send them briefly back to the world from which they came. Mississippi was a razor in the mouth, a history tucked beneath the tongue until even the saying sharpened itself on the edge of the afternoon. Mississippi is the place where, on a business trip at twenty-eight, the same age I am as I write this, my father once sunk to his knees in a tailored suit, kudzu threading the breeze at the end of a sprawling cotton field—the first he had ever seen. When I say "Mississippi" my father hears "cotton," like many Black men in America.

If you've never seen a cotton field, I don't really want to hear much from you about what Mississippi is and ain't. Row after savage row, each boll of cotton dull in the light. In the setting sun, they refuse to shine, and no number of generations can make that stop my hands from itching.

Last night I told my best friend, Noel, that I could handle going to Greenville, Mississippi, alone. He gave me a look that briefly froze the candle smoke in the air between us before calmly saying, "Tomorrow you're headed to the place they told your family never to come back to or they'd kill you; of course I'm coming with you." So we leave for Greenville from Oxford together, me riding shotgun and blasting Big K.R.I.T., as another Mississippi summer blooms beyond the window, the memory of me and Noel's first summer together tucked beneath its tongue.

Truth be told, Noel punched his Ride or Die Friendship Certification nearly ten years prior to our 2021 trip to Greenville in an almost-June with weather and unpunctuated sky just like this, the soundtracks are even a little similar. Heat bloomed over the rural Minnesota campground where Soundset 2012 was set to happen. Giddy white boys in five-panel Supreme hats and muddy Jordan flip-flops danced as bass evicted the birds from the trees.

The lineup of Soundset 2012 was an oasis of indy hip-hop, and maybe the last time Kendrick Lamar was going to show up sixth on the billing of anything. Which placed the Compton rapper a mere five spots ahead of Big K.R.I.T. The sun was gold as a fitted cap sticker, hammering down on the main stage with heat I wouldn't see again until arriving in Mississippi for the first time. & onstage I'm hearing Mississippi, for the first time, loved in a mouth like my own. & briefly, I'm in love, despite the heat which is maybe the first Mississippi ass shit I have ever done.

I watched K.R.I.T.'s matte-black chain sway and bounce against his chest like a parallel heart as we pushed closer and closer to the front through wave upon wave of Susans. The chain was a thick black disc with what I first thought was a cleaver carved out of it. In the crowd every step towards him a call to sit, smoke a spell in the shade of his voice. Because June is already throwing its weight in the windless air and we are all ready to beg for rain when K.R.I.T. is nearing the end of his set that he admits has already gone over its allotted time—but fuck it, one more song about hometowns, one more time for the choir to try and pull the clouds over the day like a veil, one more time with feeling for the Black boys whose state sits above their chest, an absence in the shape of a blade, an edge in the shape of an inheritance.

And then, that's when the bullshit started.

Midway through the very next set, Lupe Fiasco calls on the crowd to pray to a single cloud, for a little rain after a full day of 102. Within three songs that single cloud mutated behind us and swallowed the sun. And for a moment there is nothing to do but dance as the drizzle answers us. Noel looks at me and I know these are the eyes of my brother, that as Charlie Parker once said of Dizzy Gillespie, this boi is the other half of my heartbeat.

And just like that, Lupe cuts the beat off to tell us there's a tornado on the way. The concert is over.

Almost without our notice we have done what Americans do, we have prayed too hard and received what we prayed for. We thought it was a joke until Lupe sprinted offstage, sprinted back onstage to unscrew his custom-made gold-plated microphone and yam it into his jacket pocket before sprinting offstage again. We didn't know until June cracked open—above us, hail in all directions; the summer now a fury of pearls.

It is impossible for me to not think of all this as I thumb through more Big K.R.I.T. songs to add to me and Noel's playlist on the way to Greenville, to the echo of my family's own disaster in Greenville. There are maybe no better brothers than the brothers made in a shared running. I hear nothing but Big K.R.I.T. in this, the sped-up Adele sample, K.R.I.T.'s chain black as a moon in exile. How Mississippi was an absence before it was a cleaver, a drought before it was a home. How lucky to hold all of June in your voice, to rap like the heat has no authority over you—and only after you are done singing, to let the day buckle into suffocating rain.

June 2021 gilds the trees and windows of passing cars, June gilds the kudzu, and "Bury Me in Gold" by Big K.R.I.T. is rattling the car before we even reach Greenville—so June gilds the bass.

But even a Mississippi June can't gild the cotton. Cotton is where the light goes to die. It reminded me of why I've come so far to get here. And how many years it's taken. All of this to say, on the road from Greenville to Oxford, every field was loud with regret; but whose?

Let me say it plain: I have been ashamed of how long it has taken me to finally reach Greenville. There are reasons, sure. By the time I had a car in Mississippi I was already a third-year MFA candidate, a first-time author on a nation-wide tour. I was often gone from Oxford for stretches of time, days or sometimes entire weeks, and when I would get home to Mississippi I could never fathom returning to the car to drive the 270 miles back and forth to Greenville.

My grandmother was from Greenville in the way rubble is "from" a building that was once standing right there. In 2016, the news that a Black church had been burned in Green-ville found me in my university office. The burned church was spray-painted with "Vote Trump." I wrote a poem about fires, about holy, about my mother who I promised I wouldn't let myself die in Mississippi. We can pretend that's the only reason it took so long for me to get to Greenville, that excuse is as warm and inviting as a June afternoon, the door to that denial closes at the end of this paragraph; walk out.

The real reason, I know as the bass of "Bury Me in Gold" soars in from the car speakers, is that to see the town is to admit that I cannot afford to be kept alive by this story and this story alone anymore. I learned this story about my fam-ily a couple of months after I stood at the edge of a train track and decided that I did want to live, though I didn't know what for. I had never considered living for the sake of myself to be a satisfying answer.

To see Greenville, to step out of the car, is to make real the fact that there may be no remaining records of Albert Edward Leland, my great-grandfather. There may be nothing to hold that says, *Once a man lived here, he had 206 bones, his daughter became the prettiest girl in all East St. Louis.* To see Greenville was to concede that I have let my dead be my tether for far too long. I pushed all these thoughts to the back of my mind, because where else to put them? Ultimately, America is a project of terror, fueled by terror to produce more terror.

There are places in America that fill some Black folks with several generations of bass, and many of those places have been homes for other Black people for generations. It is the cradle of our laughs and heavy sighs, and in another timeline my grandmother stays a white man's daughter in the eyes of the law and maybe never arrives in St. Louis, and I am never born and there is another child at her side hearing all her tales of a childhood reeking of magnolias. I can't say she would have been happier in that world than she was in this one, but I know things would have been different.

Noel and I throttle past another cotton field, a pasture of ghosts, while K.R.I.T. hums in the choir belting, "Bury me in gold, bury me in gold / just in case I'm forsaken and I have to pay for my soul." I think about how, if you are four years old and must flee everything you've ever known, maybe "different" can be a synonym for "heaven."

I've got cotton and gold on my mind. The first piece of art I ever owned is of cotton, painted by my sister's hand. For all the years I lived in Mississippi, this was the first face I saw in the morning and often the last face I saw at night. In the portrait, Cotton Crown, a Black woman has that thousand-mile stare that makes her everyone's aunty, the crosshatches darkening her face, every brushstroke in her face is a parade of small birds. Along her left cheek a long scar twists out from her lower jaw, curling brown as wilting ivy.

The scar blooms upward until it becomes ten leaves cradling a boll of cotton. From the cotton, a crown; from the face, a sonata. I arrive in Greenville with the bass knocking, thinking of what it means to knit a crown from what once sought to destroy you. Because it's the first time I've said it and really meant it: I intend to survive Greenville.

The street we're on is a bleary stretch of plaster-white churches and low-slung houses. I've come looking for census data. City hall is mostly a bust, but recommends we check across the street at the library, where I spend the next few hours looking through three boxes of microfiche census records and wondering why exactly folks would bother to write on a census record if they weren't planning to write legibly.

Part of my great-grandfather's hustle was his penmanship, which would've shamed any of the slaveholders we carve into our currency. His penmanship was a sign to the National Life Insurance Company, where he was manager; some kinds of grace can leave you passing for white. I know this because sometimes, when I make calls looking for records of Albert Leland, I shave several octaves off my voice. I feel most colored when I sound white on the phone, and maybe he felt the same when he looked at what his hands had made and saw that the hustle was good.

None of the library records have what I'm looking for, the sun is dragging lower in the sky now, and I'm starting to feel the desperation of the moment. I've made so much of wondering what I would do if I came all this way for evidence that may well have been burned. And if not burned, lost. And if not lost, then what? The thoughts are swelling in my mind, a whole hive of my failures, when Noel comes and says that he looked up the hours for a nearby historical society. They aren't supposed to be open, but we have nothing left to lose. We trek under the sun, bleary gold cutting against our lengthening shadows.

To my surprise, after ringing the doorbell and getting no answer, we hear the door crack open. The dude who runs the place holds his thin blue medical mask over his face with one hand and asks what we're looking for. You know by now the story I told him, the truest story I know about a man threatened with wings. I want to show you the one I've never told but always considered. My answer to that question I get all the time, polished like a stone: What am I doing in Mississippi?

I came to Mississippi looking for a man swallowed in the drawl of June. He passed for white and this was his profession. I came looking for a long history of disappearing. This is the story of my great-grandfather, my grandmother's father, and in Greenville he once sold lies and allegedly faulty medical equipment.

I'm what happens to the body when the hustle goes bad. A whole town, your town, or just the pitifully few men it takes to seed a mob marched in and said, "That ain't no white man."

And there was nothing to deny. Nowhere to hide, but anywhere else.

A trickle of sweat surrenders its way down my face, I can hardly be honest for all this June.

Far as I see it, this whole town bent around a question. I'm related to that question. It's a question about how we save ourselves. But I want to find him, that man, who wasn't white but every photo named him moonlit. And that day I imagine he rose, not like a man but a promise; his return already blooming, a reverse migration that I've given my name. Three generations between then and now, between feather and mercy.

But I want you to hear me here: What if he did not flee, but spared everything the heat glazed in Greenville? What if the mercy was always his? What if I come from a long line of wings and every time I speak his name in this town, Albert Leland, the light flinches with memory? Because Mississippi remembers. Because we have good cause to remember what you got good cause to forget. Maybe "escape" was always the wrong word for an unfurling of wings.

I want to tell him this story, one I can't stop seeing. About what comes when you threaten a man with what he already was. How Albert Leland's wings unsheathed and already shined tar-black, as if they had been waiting for this threat since the floods. And as I imagine it, none of the men in the mob noticed how the light on his bald spot briefly made Albert Leland every phase of the moon before he rose, all his rage flowered like lightning within a cloud, and looked to the coast where his daughter once took uneasy steps towards a home that would never be home again. Where my grandmother touched her hand to the crest of a wave and laughed the last laugh she'd ever unbraid in Mississippi.

Is there a history that can survive this? Is this a history I can survive? What kind of ghost story am I all these miles from home?

What comes when you threaten a man with what he already was? Some call it escape, some call it obedience—and how am I different? Showing up three generations late, obeying this old threat with my new face? A lineage I almost left, me and all my sorry light.

In the greedy swelter of June, outside the Greenville Historical Society and before the silvered curl of the curator, I'm a tradition. I'm a boi doing an impression of a man, doing an impression of a man, doing an impression of a man, each of them, each of us, trying desperately not to get killed, by ourselves. I came from the smoke of a town named for the cure for smoke. I came, all this way, afraid I have lived in vain. But in the calm light, I'm alive and forgiveless. I tell him I want my records, I want Albert Leland's name anywhere.

Fuck it, I tell him aloud. *I want to survive; I want our ghost story back.*

He mostly nods somberly, cocking a gray-speckled eyebrow slightly when I mention the threat of tar and feather before shrugging in slight apology. He lets us in and takes off to the back as I take pictures of pictures my grandmother might be in the background of. Blues audiences with bone-bright smiles, men kissing their best girls on the cheek. It feels so strange to be looking at her almost-life that I barely hear the man come back with a thick tome bound in rich green leather. An old phone book and, finally, on one page: Leland, Albert (c; Jeanette; 5) mgr Natl Life Ins Co. h 701 N. Theobald.

I'm certain now that there is no way to prepare to stand on the ruins of the ruins of where your grandmother took her first steps in this world. I'm certain because in my dreams I return to 701 N. Theobald, a barren field at the end of a maze of verdant cul-de-sacs. What remained at the address was a raised concrete platform; crushed beer cans winked like shucked oysters. There was nothing to keep the air in my chest. Only the understanding that the breath was still there as I sat briefly where there might have been a porch, where my grandmother and her four siblings might have grown to imagine whole worlds, to play baseball, to call each other some names in anger and other names in grace. If. Before they built whatever has since been destroyed, she made a life here in the shadow of a lie that she didn't know was a lie until it collapsed around her and took the house with it.

A little under a year after her death, I sat there in Greenville, in the muzzle of a too-long summer, hoping that wherever she was looking from that she was looking. My great-grandfather passed from this town under a blade, the bass thudding in his chest as he bundled up his family and prepared for a long journey, towards East St. Louis and the rest of my grandmother's childhood. This life that I have not always wanted began to finally take new shape. I have many theories about when I stopped wanting to die and this isn't where any of them end because that's not really how suicidality works. I want to live today, I wanted to live yesterday. I wanted to live on June 24, 2021, the day I stood on my grandmother's demolished house three generations after a threat and felt the heat crown me before a hiccup of thunder nudged me back into the car.

When I got back into the car and we heard the engine grind to life, "Bury Me in Gold" was still playing. And you'll have to take my word for it, but just then the clouds let out an honest-to-god sun shower and if there's any way for me to leave Greenville, perhaps forever, I want to remember it just like this: a curtain of June-gilded rain, as K.R.I.T. sings the dirge that will never be all the way a dirge just the harmony that comes with the certainty that living or dead, heaven or its absence, you are headed towards your people as yourself. Let the sun-shower pummel the ground to life, let the choir swell and clap like a tide. I'm not going anywhere by my own hand.

I want acres of gold for the dead, miles of champagne for the remainder of my living.

In the glowing rain I exhaled and gunned the engine—I laughed my grandmother's laugh into the Mississippi sky until the clouds became a memory and I was finished haunting my own name.

Julian David Randall's
The Dead Don't Need Reminding Playlist

"Big K.R.I.T.," Big K.R.I.T.

"Son Of Shaft/Feel It (Live)," The Bar-Kays

"Memories," Thutmose

"Heaven Only Knows," Towkio, Chance the Rapper, Lido, Eryn
    Allen Kane

"Hide (feat. Seezyn)," Juice WRLD, Seezyn

"What's Up Danger (with Black Caviar)," Blackway, Black Caviar

"The Valley of the Shadow of Death," Mick Jenkins

"Mr Blue," Catherine Feeny

"2009," Mac Miller

"LOST IN THE CITADEL," Lil Nas X

"R.E.D.," The Halluci Nation, Yasiin Bey, Narcy, Black Bear

"Blood on Me," Sampha

"Things You Could Die For If Doing While Black," Mick Jenkins,
    Ben Hixon

"Heavenly Father," Isaiah Rashad

"Life Of The Party (with André 3000)," Kanye West, André 3000

"A Change Is Gonna Come," T-Pain

"Donuts (feat. UMI)," Isaiah Rashad, UMI

"Believe," Big K.R.I.T.

"Come My Way (feat. Krayzie Bone)," Saba, Krayzie Bone

"Under The Magnolia Tree," Pale Jay

"Never Catch Me," Flying Lotus, Kendrick Lamar

"Oldie," Odd Future

"New Level (feat. Future)," A$AP Ferg, Future

"Dreams and Nightmares," Meek Mill

"Lord Knows / Fighting Stronger," Meek Mill, Jhen Aiko, Ludwig
    Göransson

"Rug Burn," Mick Jenkins, serpentwithfeet

"Paranoia," Chance the Rapper, Nosaj Thing

"Atlas Complex," theMIND

"Survivor's Guilt (feat. G Herbo)," Saba, G Herbo

"Elevators (Me & You)," Outkast

"Mirror," Kendrick Lamar

"The Devil Is a Lie," Rick Ross, Jay-Z

"I Got 5 On It," Luniz, Michael Marshall

"Rainforest," Noname

"Redbone," Childish Gambino

"DEAD RIGHT NOW," Lil Nas X

"Goodnight + Goodluck," Tye Free

"Thugz Mansion – 7 Remix," 2Pac, Anthony Hamilton

"i," Kendrick Lamar

"afro futurism," Noname

"Instant Classic (Bonus Track)," Leikeli47

"Bury Me In Gold," Big K.R.I.T.

ACKNOWLEDGMENTS

So many ancestors' survival led me to this book, I acknowledge this before anything else.

Versions of these essays appeared in *Vibe Magazine, Black Nerd Problems, Los Angeles Review of Books,* and the anthology *Wild Tongues Can't Be Tamed.*

Thank you to the team at Bold Type who chose this book, thank you for showing me what's possible!

My forever thanks and gratitude to my incredible editor on this book, Molly McGhee. This has been, without doubt, the most difficult book I have ever written. Thank you for your vision, your tender guidance, your belief as you helped me put the pieces back together and fall back in love with what I needed to say. Without you, there is no book.

Thank you to my wonderful team of agents, Patrice Caldwell and Trinica Sampson-Vera along with the wonderful Abbie Donoghue. I am so very grateful for your advocacy and your continued belief in this book and what it could become, there is no luck like the luck that brought me friends and advocates like yall!

Thank you to my family, my dearest friends, the Mississippi where this book began, my teachers, my aces, and the West Side of Chicago; because of you, I am.

At my side through all of this, my partner, Justice. I am so very proud to love you and be loved by you, your mind is the warmest place to be.

Julian Randall is a contributor to the number-one *New York Times* bestseller *Black Boy Joy*. His middle-grade novel, *Pilar Ramirez and the Escape from Zafa*, was published in 2022. He has received fellowships from Cave Canem, Tin House, and Milkweed Editions. He is the winner of the 2019 Betty Berzon Emerging Writer Award from the Publishing Triangle, the 2019 Frederick Bock Prize, and a Pushcart prize. His poetry has been published in the *New York Times Magazine*, *Ploughshares*, and *POETRY*. His first book, *Refuse*, won the Cave Canem Poetry Prize and was a finalist for an NAACP Image Award. He lives in Chicago.